STALKING A DIVA

The Leandra Ramm Story
as told to D. Rocca

D. Rocca Reporting

A Story Told By
Leandra Ramm

STALKING A DIVA™

Black Diamond Books™
A division of Black Diamond Data, LLC
Pittsburg, California

BLACK DIAMOND BOOKS SECOND EDITION, JUNE, 2013

CREATE SPACE PRINT VERSION

https://www.stalkingadiva.com

Library of Congress Control Number: 2012946485

Ramm, Leandra
Rocca, D

Stalking a Diva/Leandra Ramm as told to D. Rocca

ISBN-13 978-0-9858383-1-7

Manufactured in the United States of America

ABOUT STALKING A DIVA

After first seeing Leandra Ramm on CNN's *Anderson Cooper*, a mentally unbalanced but seasoned cyberstalker from Singapore relentlessly pursues her, without ever having met her in the flesh. This true story follows Ramm's physical and virtual journey to free herself from an abusive predator in a climate of law enforcement inertia and apathy.

This story is a news report conducted by the author D Rocca, a lawyer from California. It is written in the first person of the heroine of the story, Leandra Ramm.

For accuracy much of this report derives from intangible communications (e.g., emails, blogs, phone recordings, chat logs). Except as otherwise interpreted, in the interest of the best representation of the facts, we let such communications speak for themselves.

We welcome comments from anyone who wishes to contribute insight into this story. You may do so at https://stalkingadiva.info

Leandra's Dedication

My story and case not only affected me and my life, but the lives and careers of many others, both personally and professionally. My heart goes out to all that were drawn into this case because of their association with me. This book highlights many of those that were involved; the ripple effect that my case had is tremendous. I want to express a sincere apology for the impact my case had on all of the lives of others that may or may not be mentioned or referenced in this book. Therefore, this book is dedicated to the many victims and survivors of cyber-stalking around the world.

To my late grandmother Ruth Rosenbluth, who believed in me even before I was born.

Our special connection was filled with laughter, love, friendship, and joy.

Her beautiful being inspires me to live my life to the fullest and soar to the top.

D. Rocca's Dedication

To "Mulle," my late maternal grandmother, an author, poet and the last scion of the Hirzel Verlag, publisher of the brothers Grimm and Goethe. She took me to my first opera in Verona's ancient amphitheater where I beheld a diva for the first time.

TABLE OF CONTENTS

PROLOGUE

According to the federal Bureau of Justice Statistics Supplemental Victimization Survey (SVS), individuals are classified as stalking victims if they experienced sending unsolicited or unwanted e-mails on at least two separate occasions. In addition, the individuals must have feared for their safety or that of a family member as a result of the course of conduct, or have experienced additional threatening behaviors that would cause a reasonable person to feel fear. This makes me a stalking victim somewhere between 3000 and 4000 times over what's required.

Although I am joined by many victims, my situation is unique in its severity, its intensity, and the sheer volume and relentlessness of the attacks. If this story were fiction, the reader would have to suspend disbelief over the course of reading it. In truth, it is all too real, beginning with my donor origins from a controversial genius sperm bank to the twisted mind of a recidivist predator, whose violence, I was certain, would infiltrate every waking moment of the rest of my natural life.

I fervently hope that Stalking a Diva brings a much needed awareness to cyberstalking and its destructive effects. My chilling experience offers a detailed education on this horrendous crime—it is my goal to put an end to it and to continue my journey free of it.

I also hope this book will convince the silent victims of cyberstalking, bullying, and cyberterrorism to find their voice, to lobby their representatives, and to shed light on a problem that our society, lawmakers, and law enforcers have, up to now, failed to validate.

PART ONE
THE PREY: LEANDRA RAMM

Profile

"My name is Leandra Ramm. I was born on July 27, 1984, in New York, New York." This story "is about my being the victim of crimes, which have occurred during the last six years, beginning in 2005 and continuing until this day."[1]

Over these six years, my persecutor has launched thousands of attacks against me, using websites, blogs, and email bombs. He has publicly labeled me a "c**t," "whore," "thief," and "prostitute" and has unearthed my most intimate vulnerabilities, while destroying a promising career. Thousands of times, he has threatened not only me, but also my family, employers, co-workers, friends, acquaintances, and even the press with death, rape, and mayhem. What makes my story unique is that I've never met or seen my abuser, but his presence in my life has been more constant than any real person's. What follows is my tale of suffering and redemption, from victim to victor.

Genius Roots

My life began eventfully. I was no ordinary infant. In fact, at the time I was born, my origins were so distinctive that only a handful of other children on earth shared them. I was the product of genius sperm and my mother's egg. But the genius sperm did not belong to the man I call my father.

After my parents' multiple attempts at beginning their own family, doctors broke the news to my dad David that he was sterile.[2] In the spring of 1983, David traveled to Italy, where my mom Adrienne, an Isadora Duncan dancer, was performing at the Uffizi Galleries in celebration of the restoration of Botticelli's *La Primavera*. He wanted to break the news to her personally.

Adrienne had always wanted a family and was certain it was her destiny to be a mother. Although it would have been devastating to just about anyone else, my parents took the opportunity to turn this apparent negative into a positive. Under their Buddhist practice, which focused on expiating and transforming negative karma, they used this great disappointment to chant, discuss their options and take positive action to overcome any obstacles. Dad knew that Mom wanted her genes to live on and wanted to experience pregnancy. He supported her fully in achieving that goal.

My mother was 33 years old and able to bear children. My parents decided on using donor sperm, which was by today's standards a procedure still in its infancy. The Repository for Germinal Choice would provide the sperm.

The Repository—3024 Sycamore Lane

The Repository was the controversial conception of Dr. Robert Graham and the recipient of the 1946 Nobel Prize in Physiology or Medicine, Hermann J. Muller. Dr. Graham was a self-made millionaire from Escondido, California, who had made his $100 million fortune inventing the plastic, shatterproof spectacle lens. He was also author of a book called *The Future of Man.* Graham believed underachievers produced too many babies and overachievers, too few. As he put it, "We seek excellence wherever we can find it."

The Repository only became viable after Muller's death and after Graham sold his lens company to 3M.[3] That was when Graham began contacting Nobelists, some of whom Muller had named as desirable donors.[4] He began recruiting donors in 1980.

Although three of the donors were Nobelists, their sperm never actually produced offspring from the Repository. Later, Graham decided that the Nobel prizewinners were too old to be donors and instead, used sperm from a group of successful scientists—Fields medalists, who were younger. The Repository used other donors, too—like professors from renowned universities and Olympic medal winners. The press dubbed the Repository the "genius sperm bank," and that name stuck.

Graham meticulously vetted and categorized donors, which was a novel concept in the '80s, where, according to my mother, choices were limited to medical students, possibly a donor sharing religious beliefs and other random markers, all of which were provided by your gynecologist. There was no verification process—you'd have to trust your doctor, who would be inseminating you, that the donor traits were true.

On the other hand, the Repository selection process was rigorous, requiring donors to answer hundreds of questions, choosing only those with high IQs and those with no "serious hereditary taint."[5]

My support of Robert Graham's vision with respect to the Repository is obviously biased, but also genuine. Had there been no Dr. Graham, I would not exist. Still, I believe that essentially, Graham wanted to help humankind by providing the best possible genetics available. Despite accusations that he was trying to create a master race, I look at Graham as a pioneer who helped infertile couples with the best start possible, the crème de la crème of insemination. He was a grandfatherly figure to me.

I met Dr. Graham numerous times before he died in 1997. Mom told me he was utterly taken by me, my enthusiasm, vitality, my musicality, and my overall energy—he found in me proof that his idea of genetic manipulation was successful. I often wonder what his opinion would have been about my autistic brother Logan, also a product of the sperm bank. Would he have found a justification about Logan's condition in my mother's age? (She was 41 when she conceived, and Graham had publicly stated that he wouldn't accept a Repository recipient aged 40 or more due to the risk of Down Syndrome.) Would he have noted Logan's savant talents as a success, perhaps an evolutionary step toward nonverbal communication?

I'll never know the answers, but my questions go to the essence of the Repository's genetic quest. In my heart and in my experience, I know that genetics alone does not create what society deems a successful human being. Nurture is a component without which I could never have withstood what was and is to come in my life. Ironically, I believe that the idea of creating a master race was one my abuser embraced and was one of the main reasons he chose me to victimize.

Adrienne Ramm, Genius Sperm Recipient

In order to get the context of who I am, I think it's important to explore the other half of my genetic material: my mother born Adrien Rosenbluth, now Adrienne Ramm.

By profession a dancer and pianist, my mother was and is a very determined woman ... courageous, too. She envisioned my birth well ahead of its occurrence. She made it happen, but not like other women.

Adrien Rosenbluth was born in 1950, the offspring of Sol, a brilliant New York attorney who struggled with tuberculosis while building his law practice, and my beloved grandmother, Ruth, who was seminal (and I mean that almost literally) in my conception.

My mother was the third of five children and grew up in Far Rockaway, New York, in a large Victorian home. The backyard garden where she often played as a little girl became the setting where she eventually wed my father, David Ramm. Before my grandfather accepted a position working for New York Supreme Court's Appellate Division, he had his private practice, and money was so tight that my grandparents took in boarders to make ends meet.

One of the tenants was an artist who transformed her living space into an art studio. Paintings, paintbrushes, and canvases were everywhere. Better yet, she had a piano. That's where my mother, as a child, taught herself to play while the artist was painting. Today, she is a professional pianist, dance accompanist, and composer.

My mother inspired my love for music.

How I Met Your Mother

My mother, hazel-eyed and brown-haired, met her future husband David at a Nichiren Buddhist meeting of the Soka Gakkai International in Manhattan in the late seventies. This particular type of Buddhism focuses on the individual's empowerment to change one's destiny, transform negative karma into positive, and to fulfill one's mission in the present and the future. Negativity is an opportunity to change things for the better. These principles were essential in my survival of the cyberterrorism I was to experience—really, without them, I doubt I would have endured.

David, several years older, was my mother's favorite suitor—she had several contenders at the time. Mom has always told me how kind, caring, and considerate David was, which has always been my experience. I think about how much he must love my mother to have raised three children with her, none of whom carried his genes but all of whom he loves unconditionally.

I suppose the biggest proof of David's spirit is the way he, who has his own severe health issues, cares for my brother Logan. Now an adult, Logan still lives with my parents; his special needs will, I suspect, always require a permanent caregiver in his life. David is the only father Logan has ever known or loved and represents the stability individuals with autism crave.

So many biological fathers have abandoned children with autism because the physical and emotional costs present a challenge they can't or won't attempt to surmount. I guess David defies the old adage about blood being thicker than water. My great-grandmother Leah recognized David's essence. Perhaps that is why she encouraged the match between her beloved granddaughter and my dad.

The Fortune Cookie

March 31, 1977 would be my mother's 27th birthday. She and David had made plans to celebrate. Meanwhile, Mom's grandmother, Leah Bauman Kerner, had a stroke in Brooklyn, undiscovered until 24 hours later. By the time of Mom's birthday, Great-grandmother Leah was at NYU Hospital, where she slipped in and out of consciousness. Mom lived on 34th Street and Park Avenue, near the hospital. Given the touch-and-go circumstances of Leah's survival, Adrienne and David planned a hospital visit before their birthday dinner date.

Although I never knew her, I'm pretty sure that I inherited aspects of Leah's personality—her perseverance, her love of theater (in her case, it was early 20th century Yiddish Theater) her work ethic, and her beautiful voice. Sasha Leah (her Hebrew name) immigrated to the United States via Ellis Island when she was only 15 years old. Her mission was to earn enough money to bring the rest of her family to America from Austria. Leah came to America on a cattle boat, where a wealthy gentleman offered her a job as a tailor on the Lower East Side. Although my great-grandmother didn't even know how to use a sewing machine, she taught herself how to sew and eventually earned enough money to bring her mother and four siblings to America. Considering their prospects in Austria under the ensuing Nazi reign, that fifteen-year-old girl arguably saved six lives and their progeny.

When David and Adrienne walked into the NYU hospital room, my great grandmother opened her eyes and saw David, whom she had only seen once before, at a Passover Seder. She opened her eyes, looked right at him, and said, "You're going to marry Adrienne." Then she slipped into semi-consciousness, during which she spoke in an odd mixture of numbers and letters. Suddenly, Leah opened her eyes again and said, "You will have a daughter. She will be beautiful and wise." Again, she drifted off, woke up, and made her third and last pronouncement, "You will name your daughter after me."

Mom felt wonderful about her grandmother's declarations and after leaving the hospital, she went to a Chinese restaurant with David, her mother (my Grandma Ruth), and father (Grandpa Sol), where they celebrated her birthday. At the end of the meal, everyone was served the traditional fortune cookie. Mom's was impossibly clairvoyant; it was as if the words had spilled from Great-grandma Leah's lips onto the thin slip of paper inside the fortune cookie: "Your daughter will be beautiful and wise." At that moment, Mom turned to my dad, who presented her with an engagement ring as a birthday present. They were engaged that night.

The next day, Adrienne bought a baby name book. Under the name "Leah" was my name, Leandra. Ultimately, I would be born under the sign of Leo, the name was also a universal tribute to Leah, who died shortly after her fall.

Phil Donahue

The *Phil Donahue Show* was really the first American talk show, later spawning an entire genre. It aired for 26 years on national television, preceded by three years of a local broadcast in Dayton, Ohio. It was broadcast nationwide between 1967 and 1996.[6] Grandma Ruth, Leah's daughter, was an avid Donahue fan.

In the Eighties, there were very few television-recording options. Video recording devices with their clumsy cassette tapes were a gamble. Maybe your VHS recorder would work, maybe not—too risky to miss a highly anticipated show. If you really wanted to catch an episode, you would watch it the day it aired. I imagine Grandma Ruth, one of my favorite people, incidentally, set up her morning, assuring that her errands were complete and her business done either before the show or during the commercial breaks.

On October 29, 1982, Donohue featured Doron Blake, an early offspring of the Repository, whom Ruth described as an adorable blond-haired, blue-eyed baby. She said he looked right into the camera and made the viewer want a baby just like that. Ruth picked up the phone, dialed the station, and ordered a transcript of the Repository show.

Repository Baby Making

In September 1983, Ruth presented the Donahue transcript to Adrienne, which contained Repository contact information. Right away, Mom called the phone number, Graham's actual home phone number. That Graham had provided this personal piece of information in a public document, especially given his vast wealth, impressed her a great deal. It showed a certain integrity and transparency and gave her confidence that she was following the right path by calling him.

After several rings, a sweet-voiced older lady answered the phone. Mom immediately opened up to the lady about her recent discovery that David was infertile. In response, the woman revealed that she was sitting in "the sewing room," which housed nine canisters of high-quality sperm. That struck my mother as odd, but endearing. The woman surprised her even further by saying, "Let me put you on the phone with Dr. Graham."

Adrienne couldn't believe she was actually talking to this renowned individual and how normal and nice he seemed. Graham initiated a type of screening, asking her what she did and a little about herself. Adrienne told Graham that she loved the arts and expressing herself and was very happy when she was in the creative mode. Then she said, "I want to do the ultimate creative act and have a baby, the best creative thing I can do."

Graham liked that response and told her, "You sound just like what we want." He then sent her and David an application and a little information about the Repository.

David and Adrienne eagerly completed the Repository application. The questions ranged from age and mother's health to talents and genetics, with marital status of "married" as a prerequisite. For extra credit, they sent Graham videos of Adrienne dancing and music she'd composed.

Dr. Graham was impressed and, after receiving her package, immediately called her. The Repository had accepted her application. Now it was Adrienne's turn to select her "mate." Graham sent her donor profiles matching each of those nine canisters in the sewing room.

Adrienne couldn't believe that this amazing sperm bank was completely nonprofit. Graham, already a millionaire, was uninterested in any form of compensation and he explained that neither were the donors. So, essentially, my parents only had to pay for the shipping and handling of the tank, which the Repository would send to her. Mom told me the cost was around $60. With my sister and brother, also products of the Repository, AIDS testing became mandated for sperm banks, which added about $500 to the overall cost. Everyone agreed that these sums were unbelievably affordable for such a priceless miracle.

There was one non-negotiable condition required by the Repository, and that was the promise that neither Adrienne nor David would attempt to contact the donors or discover their identities. Privacy was of the utmost importance for several reasons, one of which was to avoid the possibility of any financial responsibility on the part of the donor later on in the child's life. My parents readily agreed.

Fertilization Attempt, Take 1: Donor Purple

After carefully reviewing the donor profiles, David and Mom settled on Donor Purple because out of the nine offered, he seemed most physically like David: tall and slim and with brown hair and eyes. Purple even enjoyed the same hobbies as David— literature, tennis, and music. So, Purple it was. I should mention here that "purple" and all color references by the Repository signify the color of the ampoule, or "straw," in which the donor semen was frozen. The straws were an eighth of an inch in diameter and two inches long.

The Repository sent Adrienne a little kit to determine when she was ovulating and would send the tank containing the straw of semen—just enough for one fertilization attempt—to her gynecologist. Adrienne's next ovulation would begin in early October, and she had already made an appointment with her doctor to perform the procedure. Time was of the essence.

The tank arrived, and Mom brought it in a cab to the gynecologist's office on the day of the appointment for artificial insemination. After the usual niceties, the gynecologist removed some of the sperm from the tiny ampoule, which had been kept frozen with liquid nitrogen. After examining a specimen under the microscope, he shook his head. "Adrienne, I have some bad news. The sperm is dead."

The sperm was not motile; there would be no insemination from the Repository that day. My mother was very disappointed. She had waited so long and had been through a metaphorical roller coaster ride of emotions since learning about David's sterility. And now this?

Her doctor tried to comfort her by offering her sperm he could obtain that day. Adrienne would still be ovulating and, since the sperm would be from a medical student, everything would work out. Mom was shocked at the insensitivity of this offer, although she realized her doctor meant well. She knew what she wanted and it wasn't an anonymous sperm donor. It was what she and David had envisioned and what the universe had provided them—a Repository donor with a known history and great genes.

Later, Adrienne would comment that this failed first attempt was meant to be. Otherwise, I wouldn't have been born a Leo. Adrienne thanked her doctor and proceeded back home, resolved to mitigate this latest setback.

Take 2: Sperm Donor Clear

After coming back from the doctor, Adrienne immediately called the Repository, explaining to the elderly lady in the sewing room the non-motility of Donor Purple's sperm. The woman responded that nobody had been successful with Purple so far and suggested choosing another donor.

Once again, Adrienne and David reviewed the Repository list and their corresponding profiles, each of which comprised ten main pieces of information. They were all intelligent and great achievers—one in science, another in math. At this point, my parents would take any of them, as long as they were viable. Much later, David—my dad—told me that they never really sought out a "genius" baby. They just wanted a healthy, happy child.

The sewing room woman, Julianna McKillop, was director of the sperm bank in the 1980s. She told Adrienne that the Repository had had success with Donor Clear. He'd already had his own children and a few Repository pregnancies that were currently gestating. Mom agreed to Clear. This time though, the Repository would send the canister to the Ramm home instead of a doctor's office, with simple instructions on how to perform the insemination.

My parents got the tank on November 7, 1983, and I would be conceived, albeit in an unusual way, that night.

Attributes of a Genius Donor

Apart from references to his "outstanding sperm quality and high conception rate," my biological father's genetic synopsis reads somewhat like an online dating profile for the perfect man. Mr. Clear 's official one-line summary was "outstanding intellect with exceptional athletic ability." My biological dad was born in the 1940's and of Northwest European ancestry, blue eyes, fair skin and blond, curly hair "with balding." He was 5 feet 10 inches (1.8 meters), 163 pounds (74 kg), and his general appearance was "soft features with round face." His personality was "warm with good presence." He was a professor of a hard science at a major university and described in the Repository profile as producing "outstanding research."

Apparently, my birth father was not only smart, but also an athletic champion while a student at a large university in a "most demanding sport requiring exceptional coordination." To this day, I wonder what that sport was. He was too short for basketball, not beefy enough for football. And while track and field is "demanding," it doesn't require exceptional coordination, nor does swimming. Soccer, maybe, or lacrosse.

Clear was "good with children," seldom lost his temper and had "good diplomacy and tact." He enjoyed "gardening, skiing, and reading," was in excellent health, had parents in their 60's and 70's at the time of his donating, with "average age of death" for grandparents at 85. He had type O+ blood and two children whom he claimed as his own. I had another biological family! This last bit of information was a paradox in that it was comforting to know I had other biological siblings (other than Courtney and Logan Ramm), but it was fascinating to wonder who they were.

I have always wanted to meet my donor, so I could answer the essential question—Where did I come from? I have not been actively searching for him, but given the publicity I would receive on national television, I am a little surprised that his identity is still not known, and that I have not met any other of my half-siblings.

Don't get me wrong. In no way do I feel a void in my life as I have an incredible dad whom I'll always consider my father, even though he isn't genetically linked to me. Still, it would be nice to meet my biological father and see who he is, what he does professionally, and to know what we have in common. If I have the fortune to meet my donor one day, I would love to thank him for giving me life and enabling my parents to start the family they so dearly wanted.

Serendipity under the Parachute

My mother acquired a parachute while attending Bensalem College, an experimental school, aligned with Fordham University in the Bronx. An English poet, Elizabeth Sewell, conceived of the program with a close friend, one of Fordham's Jesuit priests, and it was highly selective, admitting only thirty students per year. There were no grades, no classes. The primary requisite was to have some record of your experience, but there had to be a transcript of some sort documenting the experience.

This was the late Sixties, when people liked the word "disestablishmentarianism," not only because it was rumored to be the longest word in the English language, but because of what it meant. A disestablishmentarian opposes an established order. Bensalem's curriculum and requirements were, rather, anti-requisites, allowing for the unfettered flow of ideas. In the case of my mother, the experimental program was a resounding success.

Adrienne's was a multimedia project in which she would merge film, music, theatre, and dance—an idea decades ahead of its time. She decided to incorporate a parachute in her film, purchased by her on Canal Street, after which she tie-dyed it lavender and pink.

Over the years, the parachute took on its own benevolent energy. It had a dual function at my parents' wedding, which took place at Adrienne's lovely Far Rockaway Victorian home, a place where my mother spent most of her childhood. Isadora Duncan dancers danced under the parachute, which also served as a type of "Chuppa" canopy, under which a rabbi wed my parents. Years later, I would be conceived under the parachute, as would my two half-siblings.

On the night of November 7, 1983, Adrienne and David were nervous and excited. Since they received the vial of Clear at home, they had been tirelessly envisioning me and were planning how they would perform my conception. A small pamphlet from the Repository containing instructions on insemination assisted in the more technical aspects of the conception.

This was so different from the original setting for the failed insemination by Donor Purple. My parents loved the idea of making a baby on their terms, in their home and creating an unforgettable atmosphere instead of the sterility and frigidity of a doctor's stainless steel-equipped office. Still, they had no medical background and given the failure of Donor Purple, they were apprehensive but confident. They decided to make this experience memorable and successful and created an ambience that my mother described as "angelic," visualizing me throughout their ceremony and with Bach's Brandenburg Concerti playing in the background. Mom told me later that she knew the moment she conceived.

The actual insemination, per the Repository instructions, consisted of only a few materials. First, there was the equipment, namely a speculum, a mirror, and a syringe-like device. Then, of course, the elixir—just enough semen for one "shot," so there was no room for error. Mom had used a fertility test kit in order to increase her chances of conceiving. Then it was up to David, who using the speculum to guide placement of the syringe, injected Clear's sperm right by the opening of the uterus—the entrance of her womb. Adrienne later described the precision required, as an arrow hitting a bull's-eye, an apropos metaphor, considering the visions of cupid-like cherubs she would later have. The odds were against my being created, despite the efforts my parents took to counter them. In the end only serendipity or some greater force could account for Adrienne's conception that night.

On December 7, 1983, Adrienne was to dance the Primavera (just like she did in Italy) to Gluck's opera Armide. Even though it was only one month since the Clear insemination ritual, Adrienne was confident that she had conceived under the parachute. So confident that she boldly dedicated a dance to her unborn daughter, although she had no way of knowing that she was pregnant at the time.

As she was about to enter the stage, she did a double take. Before her was what would turn out to be my spitting image in the form of a joyful little blonde cherub. Adrienne sincerely believed that I was that angel.

In the end, Adrienne's instincts were right. Two weeks after the recital, she took a home pregnancy test. It was positive.

Leandra the Leo

I was born on July 27, 1984, after a 36-hour labor, at the end of which I swallowed my meconium.

Although Mom described me as a "dream" baby, I was colicky and kept my parents up many nights with my loud crying. Maybe my strong vocal proclivity was a sign of things to come. My cooing had a lilting melody, which Adrienne described as sounding like bubbles from heaven. Mom also used the word "sparkles" to describe the noises I made. There's no doubt that my parents were in love with their baby girl.

Mom said I was the living personification of the little cherub she saw that night she devoted her dance to me, the daughter she didn't officially even know she was carrying. According to her, I was so happy to be alive and to discover all the things I could do. I walked at nine months and was dancing all the time. I was precocious and even as an infant, I had a unique perseverance, never conceding if I wanted something badly enough.

I was born under the astrological sign of Leo with my moon in Cancer and Scorpio Rising, information that was significant to Adrienne. My mother often told me that I possessed the strength of a lion combined with the warmth of the sun.

Leandra is the female derivative of the Greek mythological character Leander, whose forbidden relationship with Hero, a priestess of Aphrodite, caused him to lose his life while swimming to her in the night. Upon seeing her love Leander washed upon the shore, Hero leapt to her death from the tower to be with him.[7] Mom was moved by this tale, so it became part of my own mythology.

Ultimately, though, my name fulfills my great grandmother Leah's forecast in the Chinese restaurant seven years earlier. I was to be named after her and I was to be beautiful and wise.

Takes 3 and 4: Donor Fuchsia

When my parents wanted to have children again, Donor Clear had already sired ten children—this was apart from his own family. The Repository had a rule limiting a donor to ten children. The goal was to avoid consanguinity—the risk of two Donor siblings procreating.

My parents later decided on Donor Fuchsia, who sired my sister and brother. We later learned that Fuchsia was an Olympic Gold Medalist, whom my sister, a brilliant dancer, actually met.[8] I am happy for the connection my sister made with her biological dad, that she was able to see him and herself reflected in him.

My brother Logan is autistic and lives at home with my parents, a sweet loving young man who has trouble communicating with the world. Logan's autism is particularly important to this story because he has been a constant target of my predator, who had a penchant for victimizing those he perceived as weak.

Growing Up "Privileged" Normal

Growing up as an offspring from the Repository for Germinal Choice was very standard for me—it was all that I ever knew. I didn't know it was abnormal, or at least it didn't feel abnormal, and I attribute that to my parents and the loving and supporting home they created for us growing up. The age-old nature or nurture question was always lurking, especially in light of my own genetic roots. Which is more important? I believe both are. Your genes are your foundation, but your environment, your upbringing and childhood, is essential in manifesting your abilities. What good is a beautiful car if you are a terrible driver?

Despite my apparently privileged upbringing, my family struggled financially. Dad, a computer company systems manager for 26 years, had a good salary, but in New York City, it was difficult to support a family of five, especially given our special needs child. Dad had a heart attack at age 61; he has recovered fully and has worked from home since.

For most of my education, I attended New York public schools, including the Lab School for gifted children and The Professional Performing Arts School. Eventually, I managed to get a full scholarship at an elite private school, the Rudolf Steiner School, because of my musical abilities.

Later, relying on loans and grants, my sister Courtney studied ballet intensively at the School of American Ballet, and I went to the Manhattan School of Music Preparatory Division in high school and other private arts classes.

While growing up, I did a lot of acting, singing, dancing, and music. My mom said I sang before I spoke. I played the flute in an interschool orchestra, was in a children's choir that toured internationally, auditioned for commercials, and made TV appearances.

I can honestly say that, aside from my personal aspiration to be a world-class entertainer, my childhood was safe, warm, and loving. Yes, I had the drive to succeed, but it was tempered with my parents' reasonableness and "glass half-full" mentality. My parents never pushed me, they inspired me. In addition, I had my own ambition, manifested by my drive and passion for the arts. Yes, I was looking for a nod from society, but more than that for success that came from within. I knew I was talented and good. No one could take that away from me. Or so I thought.

As in most stories about the triumph of human spirit, I never realized how wonderful my life was until a man whom I never met stole it from me.

Finding my Talent

In second grade, I was in the school talent show. I prepared an original dance to Vivaldi's "Winter," wearing a beautiful white silk tunic that had been my mother's. Right before I went onstage, the seven-year old before me sang "The Greatest Love of All," Whitney Houston's big hit. I was standing in the wings listening to her and thought, *Hey, I can do that! I should be a singer!* I thought it was so cool, and it lit a spark in me to investigate this singing thing.

Several years later, I was in The Young People's Chorus of New York City. We performed multiple times a year and toured internationally. When I was fourteen, I was selected from the chorus to represent not only our chorus but also the entire United States in the solo vocal category of an International Choir Competition. I won the entire competition. This event was key in validating my talent from the world in general.

From a more personal perspective, my mother and her cadre of talented friends schooled me. My mother's mentor in dance was Julia Levine who was the leading exponent of Isadora Duncan's legacy. Julia was very close to our family. I confided in her one day that I didn't know what to do with my life. I loved everything: singing, dancing, acting, and playing the flute. I learned early that having many talents is a hindrance to pursuing just one. We were walking along the East River in New York City, and I remember very clearly her asking me what I loved the most. I said I loved to sing. "Then sing," she said, "and be the best singer you can be. Focus on one thing, the thing you love the most and be the best you can be at it."

Man's Rejection is God's Protection

Two memories were crucial in my decision to pursue singing, as opposed to dancing or becoming a flautist. In retrospect, they were isolated incidents. Had I been destined to pursue them, they might not have had the impact on me that they did. I still believe these experiences happened to protect me from making the wrong career choice.

When I was about ten years old, I remember being in the living room with my younger sister, Courtney, when a family friend, Marta, visited. Marta had been a superb ballerina in her youth and was now mother to a prima ballerina. My sister and I were doing ballet for her, and Marta said, "I'm sorry, but this one [pointing at Courtney] is much more talented than this one [pointing at me]."

When I was seriously considering becoming a flautist, at around fifteen, I went to see a famous flautist perform in Manhattan. I was so excited to meet her afterward! I revered her. What's more, she played a piece in her recital that I too had played! Amidst the crowed I raised my voice and said, "I loved your performance! I play the flute too, and I play that same Gluck solo for flute from *Orpheus and Eurydice!*"

She laughed at me, and scoffed, "You do?!" It was traumatizing. To this day, I remember the demeaning look she gave me. That experience greatly influenced my decision not to play the flute professionally.

Although I continued to play the flute and dance (I even went on pointe in ballet and studied up to five times a week), everything was pointing me in the direction of singing. It was the art form that I loved the most, and was the most talented at.

Competitions and Conservatories

After I won the international Choir Competition, I started taking private classical voice lessons from a mother of one of the children in the chorus. A couple of months later, I had fallen in love with classical singing. In my teens, I auditioned for Juilliard, which put me on the waiting list. I also auditioned for The Manhattan School of Music (MSM), which accepted me. I was heartbroken about Juilliard, but although I didn't know it at the time, it was a blessing to attend Manhattan School of Music. It was under an MSM teacher that I learned an amazing vocal technique, which completely transformed my method of singing. I was so inspired that I started practicing all the time, my voice improving at a rapid rate. I was singing in many different languages and my tone was developing brilliantly.

About two years later (when I was still in high school), I auditioned for Juilliard again. This time they not only accepted me, but also offered me a scholarship.

At age 20, the Sarasota Opera Apprentice Program accepted me as one of their youngest apprentices ever. I took a leave of absence from Manhattan School of Music and instead performed professionally as a young artist around the country for the next three years. I never went back to school, and I never looked back. In those two years, I worked with Des Moines Metro Opera, Toledo Opera, Arizona Opera, Opera Carolina, and others. I also had the fortune to be represented by a very well respected opera management company, Robert Gilder & Company.

Anderson Cooper—My Big Break

My stalker first saw me on CNN's *Anderson Cooper* in November, 2005. The segment covered David Plotz's *The Genius Factory*, a book about the Repository for Germinal Choice offspring. The Nobel sperm bank closed in 1999, and the records were sealed. Plotz's mission was to locate offspring and determine whether Graham's vision was a success. Did genius genes spawn a generation of geniuses?

Anderson featured me as one of an estimated 235 children born from the Repository. I was an exemplar of what the sperm bank aspired to produce, an internationally acclaimed rising star.

My milieu was opera and Plotz described me as "extraordinary." Anderson played several clips of me, walking with my dad along the East River, Roosevelt Island side, playing the piano, and singing Rossini's "Una Voce Poco Fa," from *Il Barbiere di Siviglia*. It was the break I was looking for. Right after the broadcast, I was on an emotional high. I felt the sky was the limit, confident and unbeatable. It was at this point in my emotional vulnerability, which accompanies the flush of this type of success, that my stalker Colin contacted me, using the New Jersey Opera Theatre as his conduit.

Performing Arts Culture

In performing arts, specifically the world of opera, there are many talented, well-trained, and beautiful people. Somehow, you must differentiate yourself from the competition, stand out in some way. The music academies drum into our heads that in opera, we performers will hear rejection over and over again. We should appreciate offers, not question them, because they don't come very often.

The opera community was small, so civility bordering on obsequiousness was a necessity, always. I learned later that even adhering to these rules of professional etiquette would not protect me from becoming an outcast; in fact, they would facilitate the disintegration of my career.

Neither the Manhattan School of Music nor all my professional training provided guidance on how to vet one's opportunities or benefactors. As a result, we didn't know when to consider an offer or from what we should back away.

Although the recognition I got by appearing on CNN was not specifically for my singing, doing the show was an opportunity. Anderson Cooper gave me my fifteen minutes of fame, and I wasn't going to question whether this was the best way to promote my opera career. I would receive international recognition, some of which would be for my talent. As I had been taught, I was thankful for this unique chance to shine.

Looking back, I realize how naïve I was at the time of the Anderson Cooper taping. Even then, an online search of my name would lead anyone to my personal phone number, email, and parents' address. I didn't consider exploring the potential ramifications of this very personal exposure.

As quickly as technological capabilities change, it's important to note that this occurred before the Internet and social media really expanded. It wasn't the case that I was exceptionally naïve—most of the population was, and still   is.

PART TWO
STALKER

Criminal Past

When Colin Mak Yew Loong and I first metaphorically met—I've never seen or been physically near him—he was in the throes of an international arms dealing criminal investigation originating in Singapore. I didn't know that when we first spoke.

The Singapore police already knew Mak as a harasser and serial stalker, for which he had served probation of up to two, three, or four years—no jail time.

Colin was an experienced computer stalker, relishing his time in the virtual world, where he could assume multiple identities, and stalk and threaten real people, a practice he had enjoyed since the last millennium. In 1999, when, to most of us, a Web page was a new and strange concept, Colin was actively scouring the Internet for victims, emailing, posting content, sometimes under his "real" name, sometimes using another identity, Warbird5k, Fritz Tang, Fritz Tan, Miggy, stormorochalie,[9] jasmine cardozi, jassmbrahmos, and countless variations.

Mak proved early that, regardless of the location, there were no real criminal repercussions for what he did. He had little motivation to stop doing it.

Ivy League—Harvard and Beyond

Colin's American legal troubles began more than a decade before our initial contact, while he was in the states on a student visa.

On September 26, 2000, at 12:30 in the morning, Harvard University Police arrested Mak for trespassing after a student reported him sleeping in the Lowell House basement. Worse, Harvard had already given him several trespass warnings and had arrested him fourteen days earlier.[10]

A private investigator later told me that Colin had been a university student in the United States from 1999 through 2001, attending Oberlin College in Ohio, Harvard, Northwestern, and Boston University. The United States government deported Colin back to Singapore in 2002 after his visa expired. But not before Colin had victimized others in the United States, where he lived illegally.

Under condition of anonymity, "Melissa," one of Colin's early U.S. victims, recently contacted A.J. Fardella after seeing an online version of the *Contra Costa Times* article "Tech-savvy sleuth fights for cybercrime victims."[11] The victim, now an attorney, had been a sixteen-year-old Harvard freshman in the early 2000's, interested in theater. After seeing her in a theatrical production, Colin, passing himself off as a photographer, offered to do her portfolio. She was displeased with his work and attempted to terminate their acquaintance. Unfortunately, she had provided Colin with her email address and other personal information, which Colin used to batter her with "creepy" emails of a sexual and violent nature. Despite never having responded to even one, Melissa claims that, to this day, Colin continues to harass her.

In one of my 2010 forced chat sessions with Colin, a/k/a warbird5k, he revealed problems with another co-ed at another prestigious school—Ohio's Oberlin College.

warbird5k: why do so many American women react strangely to men

I was weirded out in Oberlin where I was first at.

me: I don't know but that's no reason for you to go insane on people just because you don't like their culture

warbird5k: especially with that violinist I told you about—she—Mirabai Weihsmehl said I was inappropriate when I secured the interview with Katie Baker who was the concert mistress
I did not even talk to Mirabai about anything other than string music and that I wanted to interview her for my project paper on music
why do so many American men complain to me that they want Asian women after being treated the same way by American women?

me: I don't know
I have to go to bed soon

warbird5k: why is American culture always so confrontational towards 'aliens' and foreigners?
hmmm
but I have learnt to accept them as such[12]

me: ok

It's unclear whether Colin attended any school for a significant amount of time, or whether he ever actually enrolled in classes, although he called Oberlin his "first school in 1997."[13]

Still, he often referred to his powerful college friends, including a Chinese doctor he supposedly met while at Stanford, to gain trust and bolster his dubious educational claims. This became a familiar Colin tactic, peppering lies with just enough truth to lend his stories some credibility. Not surprisingly, he was successful at inserting himself into the lives of a vulnerable sector of society—college freshman co-eds. Lonely, homesick teenagers, away from family for the first time, rife with insecurities and anxiety were perfect pickings for a conman predator.

While he preyed on the women, he bonded with the men. One of them was Brian Asparro, a graduate student at Northwestern, whom Colin enlisted about a decade later, to visit my parents' home, uninvited.

How I "Met" My Stalker

Well, actually we never met.

A few days after the *Anderson Cooper* broadcast, a staff member at New Jersey Opera Theater called me. I had recently covered the role of Rosina in NJOT's production of *Il Barbiere di Sivigila*.

Back then, I worked directly with clients, employers, and sponsors—I didn't yet have professional representation to filter and analyze my professional choices. As my own promoter, I published my email address and phone number on Internet casting Web sites.

My stalker had contacted the New Jersey Opera Theater, falsely identifying himself as the director of the Singapore Music Festival. He had seen me singing on *Anderson Cooper* and wanted me to perform in Singapore. NJOT considered this man, Colin Mak, a valid lead to an opportunity I should pursue.

Music school taught aspiring opera singers to be grateful and ingratiating, but not how to distinguish a true opportunity from a scam. So few opportunities existed in opera that the attitude was "carpe diem," not "caveat emptor" or any other type of judicious approach. Throwing caution to the wind, NJOT hadn't even performed a cursory background search on Mak at the time they presented me with his unique "opportunity." Had they done so, they surely would not have recommended that I contact this man with a past in trespassing, harassment, and stalking, currently on trial for gunrunning.

Relying on the Opera's "referral," I called Mr. Mak in November 2005, at the phone number given to me by the New Jersey Opera staff. As well as I could discern, given my limited experience, Colin sounded legitimate, meaning he used the right terminology and seemed to know a little something about opera. His English was excellent and that he spoke with an Asian tonality and accent consistent with his assertions of being a native of Singapore. I would later learn that his nationality was one of the few truths he would reveal about himself, embedded in a heap of lies.

Mak confirmed that he had indeed seen me on *Anderson Cooper,* was mightily impressed, and planned to make me an international star. In December, I mailed "Colin M" my headshot, resume, and DVD to a designated address in Singapore.

Per his request, I also sent a PR package to Michael Fine, a reputable music producer in the Los Angeles area, now residing in the Netherlands, with whom Colin claimed to be a "colleague" and "music producer friend." I never heard back from Fine.[14]

Austrian Overtures

In early 2006, contact with Colin was sporadic, although we had begun discussions about his sponsoring my singing career. In the world of opera, or professional musicians, generally, it has always been commonplace for patrons to sponsor artists financially. Mozart and Chopin were "kept" by aristocracy, sometimes royalty, and even anonymous donors. Colin cleverly used his knowledge of patronage in the arts to insinuate himself more permanently into my life.

The Austria idea began while I was still a student at Manhattan School of Music. My voice teacher spoke highly of it and of Esther Hardeburgh, who ran the program. My voice teacher was on the faculty for the summer opera program in Salzburg run by The University of Miami. The costs, though, were prohibitive, and a previous funding arrangement had not panned out. As he was always boasting about money and offering it, I asked Mak if he would pay for the program, figuring that "no" would be the worst possible outcome. I wasn't about to miss an opportunity simply by not asking for it!

He wrote:

"Darling... if you cannot make full payment for your summer term in Salzburg—tell me please. I will make an effort to pay it for you."[15]

On that promise, I began preparing in earnest for the upcoming summer program; there was little time to lose and deadlines were looming. I contacted program heads, prepared repertoires, studied German, and discussed curricula.

In the meantime, Colin was actively making other Austrian plans, a diversionary move to distract me from his failure to pay my tuition at Salzburg, something he had never intended to do. Instead, he was putting together a deal for me to sing at Schonbrunn, in Vienna. This was an entirely different scenario and venue from the Salzburg program. Still, I was under pressure and followed his directions, sending photos and repertoires to both the Schonbrunn lead and to Salzburg.

By keeping me busy and distracted, Colin was effective, for a while at least, in forestalling my inevitable questions about the as-yet-unpaid tuition for Salzburg.[16]

Doubt and Disappointment

In late June of 2006, with the deadline for payment having passed, I sent Colin an email requesting payment status.

"I hope you will be able to pay on Tuesday because we are passed (sic) the deadline."

Colin wrote me back a few hours later:

well sorry I was staying at a friend's place over the last 48 hrs.
talking business as well as personal things.
the slow money transmission time is because I am using profits from a deal to pay both your airfare as well as the tuition fee. the client was slow in wiring funds from Hong Kong.
I hope you are well. I am still nursing the muscle injury which is causing me discomfort even when I try to sleep but other than that... I am very blessed.[17]

This response should have struck me as suspicious. Its petulant and evasive tone was inappropriately familiar, a foreshadowing of the new dynamic we would share later on.

I was too intent on not losing Salzburg to notice these details. An artist's focus has to be pure and unwavering. It's a meditative hustle—the rest of the world dissipates while working or, in my case, while pursuing work. The same was true for me off the stage, when it came to furthering my art. Perhaps that is why I ignored the portentous signals emitted by my "benefactor."

From: Colin MaK warbird5k
To: Leandra Erin Ramm leandraramm
Sent: Mon, 26 Jun 2006 17:26:59 -0700 (PDT)
Subject: (no subject)

Leandra
money is not in my account yet. Client is slow.
I don't know Leandra
I need to give you a call later tomorrow-- to say whether or not we are going ahead with Salzburg.
cannot keep Dr. Hardenburgh waiting forever.
the other plans we have are still on.
I will do my best to pull this off.

Colin MaK

I wrote him back, devastated at the prospect of losing this chance, but continuing to ingratiate myself—an old habit from music school days.

Dear Colin,

Thank you for the update, although I am very sorry to hear about the possibility of this not going through. I know the program's administration and faculty will be very disappointed if I cancel this late in the game especially with all of the efforts we've made thus far. At this point, it will be very embarrassing for me to cancel as I have been in constant contact with Dr. Hardenbergh and my teacher who is on faculty there while I've been rigorously preparing repertoire and the German language itself. I appreciate everything you can do to settle this so that I may still be able to attend. I trust you will be in touch as soon as you know anything.

My deepest appreciation,

Leandra[18]

Shortly after, I reluctantly gave up the Salzburg dream and, feeling humiliated and ashamed, notified the program director I wouldn't be attending. Meanwhile, Colin was still promising to pay and I, employing the "appreciate your opportunities," dynamic imparted as part of my musical training, was still thanking him.

Audition at the Violin Shop

I had been completely absorbed with Austria, but Colin had other plans for me, which he cleverly intermingled with the Salzburg dialogues. He was intent on my auditioning for a friend of his in Manhattan.

It began with a February email from Colin to Gregory Singer, proprietor of Gregory Singer Fine Violins, on Manhattan's Upper West Side.

"HI Gregory
My friend Leandra---an Opera Singer form NYC has agreed to do a recital at your violin shop's recital hall! ...Would you like to speak with her for a while? Leandra is beautiful and has been feature on CNN, ABC News as a test-tube "Genius Baby" I will be recording her with Michael Fine soon...[19]

Colin MaK
"Allegro Con Brio!"[20]

The audition came up again on April 28, 2006.

By the time you read this—I would have sent your present—a little something form Chanel to Gregory's violin shop...collect it there
I am "forcing" you to meet him...heh heh

--Colin MaK

Beneath the text, Colin inserted a quotation ascribed to Aaron Copeland. Over the years, these pithy aphorisms from Pablo Casals to Beethoven became a recognizable characteristic of Colin's email signature.

Even though it seemed odd, I followed up with the audition at Gregory Singer's violin shop in May, 2006. My instincts were correct—it turned out to be the strangest audition of my life, beginning with the fact that I was auditioning by proxy. Colin would not be there. Ironically, I was to sing for a man named Singer.

Because I really didn't know what to expect, I went with a male friend (he was my protection) to Singer's store in Manhattan. Singer, a slight, graying man around fifty years old, greeted me and led me into the store, filled with rare and beautiful violins. He introduced me to his silent companion, a demure Asian woman, who appeared only slightly older than myself.

The bizarre circumstances led me to ask Singer, rather bluntly, about his relationship with Colin. Singer told me, vaguely, that he had met Mak in Asia, but that he didn't know Colin very well. That was strange. Why would a man, twin brother of an acclaimed actress[21] and himself an accomplished musician, with impressive Hollywood connections, be doing this favor for Colin? My optimistic side, however, convinced me that Colin must have clout in the world of classical music.

Before the audition, Singer made a strange comment. Since Colin couldn't meet me himself, Singer was to report back to Colin on whether I was attractive. Then he said, "So obviously you are, and I'll tell him that."

As odd as that remark was, it was Singer's next remark that really threw me. "Colin will probably want some type of relationship with you, but don't worry ... he's harmless." At that point, my internal alert system shifted into a higher gear, questioning the appropriateness of the conversation, the strangeness of this audition, and Singer's motivation to conduct it. On the other hand, I had my "bodyguard" with me, and there could be a career opportunity in this bizarre scenario.

I went through with the audition, in the shop's gallery area, determined to give the best performance I could. I sang an aria for him, "Una voce poco fa" from *Il Barbiere di Siviglia*, after which he said, "Phenomenal. You are terrific!" and that I passed the audition.

Audition Post-Mortem

After the audition, Singer presented me with some sample perfume—the kind you get for free in a department store, as gifts from Colin.[22] I took the testers and got out of the shop as quickly as I could. It was all too strange. But, I justified, this could all be part of my sponsor's quirkiness. After all, "the business" was rife with overreaching and harassment of vulnerable artists looking for a break. At least I wasn't facing the proverbial casting couch—what harm could someone do who wasn't even in the country?

In retrospect, these thoughts were achingly ironic. What harm, indeed? But in the Singer violin shop, at the very young and naïve stage in my professional development, I was determined to succeed. I could live with these small inconveniences and would not let Colin's schoolboy crush stop my momentum.

I neither took Singer up on his subsequent offer of performing a recital at his store, nor did I ever return to the shop.

By sheer accident, however, I saw Singer again in 2007 on the New York subway. That encounter would be the trigger for my temporary solution to Colin's stalking—the commencement of my "at-bay period."

PART THREE
STALKING STARTING

Cease and Desist Disaster

The Salzburg debacle was disheartening, and the audition bizarre, but still I didn't sever ties with Colin in the summer of 2006. I didn't really need to—his correspondence with me had dwindled somewhat; maybe his interest was waning. Later, I would surmise that Colin's apparent ebb in interest during this period was due to a simultaneous, high-profile criminal prosecution in Singapore with Colin as the defendant.

In early 2007, I was dating a tenor, Michael Wade Lee (a/k/a "MWL"), whom I had met while working at New York's Chelsea Opera Company a couple of years earlier.

As a couple, we obviously shared confidences. For me, of course, the most prevalent issue since meeting Mike was how to handle Colin's increasing attention, especially now that I realized he was a fraud and would never further my career.

I remember that Mike and I were talking casually and, I mentioned, intimately, about Colin's apparent instability and stalking tendencies. Acting on that information, and, I suspect, having done some online searching of his own, Michael sent Colin a blistering cease-and-desist communication from my computer and email account while I was out of the room, an action which infuriated me. I knew instinctively that Colin would not take such a communication lightly. And from what I had been told by Singer and the tone of Colin's communications with me, Colin considered me his "girlfriend." I also knew that Colin had outsmarted or used innocent people, and that provoking him was like teasing a snake—something one just shouldn't do.

To this day, I smart at the thought of Michael using our intimate discussions to recklessly speak on my behalf, from my America Online account, no less! I was no damsel in distress and this was not an opera libretto, where the hero tenor rescues his mezzo-soprano. I think Michael meant well, but was at once arrogant and naïve in thinking that he could stop Colin's communications. Michael would soon learn firsthand of Colin's wrath unleashed, another possibility that he had not contemplated in his hasty action.

On January 17, 2007, MWL, describing himself as my "fiancé," to show Colin I was "taken," spontaneously sent another cease-and-desist letter to Colin and "Tony," Colin's business associate in the Swedish company Protec Consulting.

Colin and "Tony" had been emailing Chelsea Opera and Opera Carolina, asking about me, potentially jeopardizing my future with them and other companies. The opera world was small; shunning by one company pretty much ended my prospects.

In response, Michael wrote the first of two cease-and-desist letters. This one was very civil-tongued and appreciative, the mark of a performer looking to keep opportunities open:

Mr. Thille and Mr. Mak,

My name is Michael Lee and I am the fiancé of Leandra Ramm. I am writing on her behalf, at her request, in order for you both to understand that you need to cease contact with Leandra Ramm.

Mr. Thille , it was VERY inappropriate to email an opera company that Ms. Ramm has worked for to try to find her like you did. You have put her in a very awkward situation with that company. That company may never hire her again because of your letter. No one wants an apology for your actions. It is enough to know that you will never do that again. We do want to know if either of you have contacted any other opera company, any musical venue, or any orchestra besides Opera Carolina and Chelsea Opera either on her behalf or looking for her. Please let me know at my return address, mikelee70, and we will take appropriate action. To repeat and clarify, please let me know if either of you has had any contact with any other musical venue BESIDES Opera Carolina or Chelsea Opera in regards to Leandra Ramm. Please reply ONLY to mikelee

Mr. Mak, please stop trying to promote Ms. Ramm. She has an agent and does not wish for you to promote her in any way any more.

STALKING A DIVA

We ask the both of you, Mr. Thille AND Mr. Mak, to cease any and all contact with any opera company ever again with regards to Leandra Ramm.

Mr. Mak, while Ms. Ramm appreciates your ...support and your generous gifts of the past, she no longer wishes to receive anything else from you, be it financially or in the form of gifts. We wish any further effort of yours to contact or promote Leandra Ramm to cease now. You, your past emails, and your newsworthy actions have made her feel very uncomfortable, and dreadfully unsafe. It is clear that you lied to Ms. Ramm of your whereabouts and why. While we understand why you may have lied, we both feel serious concern for her health and safety because of your newsworthy actions. We do not wish to be involved with either of you at all.

Mr. Mak, because you also told Ms. Ramm of your intention to visit her in North Carolina uninvited and unwanted, we want you to know clearly that she does not wish to meet you, and will never ever want any kind of relationship with you. We are both aware of what information about you has been in the news. And, at this point, because of Mr. Thille and your history, we now wish for you to stop any and all contact with her, via ANY form of communication ever again. She is now very afraid of you and concerned for her health and well being.

I am writing on her behalf, the behalf of her family and my own behalf, out of concern for her safety and security.

Please cease any and all contact with Leandra Ramm.

Any further contact will be given to the police and reported as harassment. If either of us feel threatened or harassed in any way, we will not hesitate to involve American Government Authorities.

Michael Lee [23]

Several hours later, Tony Thille responded. From the following email, we would conclude that the "Tony" who contacted my employers was likely Colin using one of his favorite tactics, spoofing an identity. The Tony Thille below appeared to be authentic. We had no way of verifying his identity, other than to compare syntax and tone (and email addresses) with ones we had received previously.

Dear Mr. Lee.

My sincere apologies.

First of all, I have not contacted any other opera company and musical venue at all, and I am not mailing on behalf of Mr. Mak. I have no intention to harass Ms. Ramm at all.

61

The thing is that Mr. Mak is possibly in the US. For the moment and he owes me a large sum of money (debts.) because of previous business, but he has stated

All the time earlier that he is romantically involved with Ms. Ramm, so that is simply why I made this enquiry as I didn't had her direct e-mail address and, cant reach him in Singapore.

So that is simply why I am trying to reach Mr. Mak through Ms. Ramm nothing else, to know his (Mr. Mak's) location if possible to take appropriate legal action against him.

Now after your reply e-mail I have the true picture clear concerning Mr. Mak, that he is a liar and probably in great need of urgent physiological help.

Once again my sincere apologies for this.

Best Regards.
Tony Thille. [24]

Colin then conveniently jumps into the email discussion, feigning ignorance, but more likely the instigator, engineering the dialogue. The "camp" to which Colin refers was, more likely, a Singapore prison and Colin an inmate for international arms dealing.

I was away at my army camp for 2 weeks
my partner in Sweden was so worried that he called you...
i did not tell him u are my GF
also his English is not perfect.... its broken
just exactly what is going on? [25]

Suspecting that Colin had duped Thille, Lee's final cease-and-desist email was to Colin alone, the civil tone replaced by anger.

Mr. Mak,

you obviously have not gotten the picture.

I was with Ms. Ramm today both times you called. We are now going to the police to file charges of harassment against you. We have asked you to cease all contact. You have not ceased contact. We will bring any and all evidence we have to the New York Police Department.

If you ever appear where Ms. Ramm or I or any of her family are, we will call the police and have you arrested.

STALKING A DIVA

Do not send money to Ms. Ramm. She does not want anything from you. Do not send gifts to Ms. Ramm. Do not come to anywhere Ms. Ramm is. Stay far, FAR away from her. She does not want anything to do with you anymore.

Leave Ms. Ramm alone. Leave her in peace. You have lied to her. You have also lied to Mr. Thille. You are a liar. You have broken Ms. Ramm's trust. You are now untrustworthy. You do not have a relationship with Ms. Ramm. You never did. You do not have anything anymore with Ms. Ramm. What little you may have had in the past is now over because of your lack of respect. Ms. Ramm does not feel safe in her own home or work place anymore because of you. You need to leave her alone. You need to stop calling. You need to forget her and move on with your life elsewhere.

Do not respond to this message. Just leave her alone and leave us alone.[26]

Arms Dealing and Emailing:
The Secret Life of Warbird5k

Up until Michael Lee sent the cease-and-desist letter, Colin had emailed me from his email address, warbird5k. Who was this "warbird," and why would this be the email address of a Singapore music producer? These were questions I never explored or even recognized, attributing them to eccentricity or some inside joke to which I was not privy.

In a twist worthy of a John le Carré thriller, we learned that Colin the Singapore music producer was a front for a much stranger, more sinister persona.

An October 2006 press release from Singapore Customs summarized Colin's predicament in a few terse paragraphs. Chaandrran was his co-conspirator, as was Tony Thille.

> "On 11 October 2006, B R Chaandrran , 45, was found guilty and convicted for abetting the unauthorized brokering of 20,000 AKMS rifles. Sentencing will be passed on 14 November 2006 at 9 am at Court 7.
>
> Singapore Customs' investigations revealed that between May to September 2005, Chaandrran, who is not a registered broker with Singapore Customs, arranged for the procurement of 20,000 AKMS rifles, valued at US$3,400,000, from a Bulgaria supplier to Syria. He was charged in the Subordinate Courts on 28 December 2005, for abetting the brokering of strategic goods in violation of the Strategic Goods (Control) Act
>
> Another person Mak Yew Loong, Colin, 30, a managing director of Protec Consulting, was also charged in conjunction with this case. Mak was sentenced to 9 months' jail on 7 July 2006."[27]

Colin had the singular distinction of being the first Singaporean sentenced under Singapore's Strategic Goods

Control Act. My stalker was an arms dealer. Could this story get any more surreal?

The Trial

The arms dealing story had been in the news months before. In July, 2006, Valarie Tan of Channel News Asia reported that Colin had received nine months' jail for trying to supply guns worth "some $5 million to Syria," that Singapore Customs officials, acting on a tip, had caught Colin in 2005 and that investigators found documents in his home, including invoices detailing a deal of $3 million worth of military assault rifles from Bulgaria to Syria.

Mak's defense counsel argued that Colin was just a pawn of Protec Consulting's CEO Tony Thille.[28] The court disagreed, unwilling to downplay Mak's role in the crime, supported by the emails investigators found on his computer.

In one such email, Mak wrote,

"The last thing we need is trouble from the Israelis and the Swedish intelligence," which the court found persuasive in showing that Colin was aware of the deal and the danger involved.[29]

In another, Colin claimed he was "already very stressed out by the gangster threats from the Bulgarians."[30] The court agreed with the prosecution that these emails proved Mak was not an innocent pawn. The latter email, in fact, showed that the buyer of the weapons had a shady background, implying that the deal was not legitimate.

Ironically, Mak's emails were the primary evidence used to convict him. There were no guns actually exchanged or seized, and no evidence showing he had profited from the deal. Instead, Colin's emailed promise to supply 20,000 guns was the prosecution's lynchpin. District Judge Wong Keen Onn considered that number too huge to ignore, finding that what Colin did could lead to such weapons falling into the hands of terrorists who would use them to kill.

STALKING A DIVA

Tony Thille emailed MWL, in broken, error-filled English, explaining his side of the arms dealing case and providing some insight into Colin's character.

Dear Mr. Lee.

I was never convicted of any felony in court together with Mr. Colin Mak and Mr.Channdrran of Dannhauser International.

How come do you think ???, I will tell you why –

I was cooperating with US. Intel and Israeli Intel from the beginning as I have strong ties to Israel, so no weapons would never ever have come in any Syrian hands, they where set up (Dannhauser and The Syrians) with US. And Israeli Authorities from the beginning (day one).

Mr. Mak and Mr.Channdrran[31] didn't know that I where an Intel infiltrator from the beginning, and was prepared to go along with this arms deal

Of pure greed only I told him (Mr. Mak) this just before the bust vent down, and what does he do go to Singapore Intel and get busted himself by share stupidity.

I tried to save Mr. Mak, but as he can't keep his mouth shut towards reporters etc. so we ended up in all the newspapers, then Singapore Customs wanted to make an example of him because of the publicity and sentenced him to jail, if he would have kept his mouth shut nothing would have happened with him.

I can fully understand the fear towards Mr. Mak from Ms. Ramm, this man is sick and need (sic) professional help, and he could possibly be in the US. now. (Just want to inform you simply)

Just wanted to explain and set the fact strait and after this now, none of you will hear from me further again ever, I can promise you this.

But Please Mr. Lee do not insult me by treating me as a simple criminal (something the cat dragged in), everybody is not rich famous stars or rich producers or beneficiaries but have to work as Business men or other unglamorous jobs to earn their living such as myself.

I Wish you and Ms. Ramm all the best of luck and success in the future.

Tony Thille[32]

The Thille email[33] alerted MWL that Colin was not what he seemed. Whether Tony Thille wrote the email, or on what level he existed was uncertain. Either way, however, I was learning a rather existential lesson about Colin. Where he was concerned, the concept of reality became very murky.

Post-Conviction Damage Control

Once Colin knew that I knew about his arms brokering conviction, he launched into full damage control mode, beginning with a phone call by one of his minions, Mona Hanson, a Virginia attorney , proclaiming his innocence.

Colin liked to convince himself that the real reason I severed ties with him was his arms dealing conviction, so he set out to convince me that he was innocent. He claimed (with some support in the press) that most of the evidence in the Singapore trial was circumstantial and no weapons were ever found. The authorities relied on email correspondence found on Colin's computer and receipts or bills of lading for a weapons shipment. Significantly, the law in Singapore was new and the prosecutor ambitious. In fact, the conviction was just more evidence against Colin's character, and I really didn't care whether his own superior grifting skills earned him an unwarranted felony conviction.

In one document titled "Dear AG Office,"[34] Colin went into an elaborate explanation on the background of the arms deal, referring to it as a "sham." Late in January 2007, he explained that he was back from a spa resort in Northern Thailand, where he supposedly met a CIA representative and his attorney. The implication was that rather than jail, he was in Thailand at some swanky resort to negotiate favorable treatment for his arms dealing conviction. Mona Hanson would later tell me that Colin had boasted about getting his visa to the United States renewed based on his heroic actions in getting the *real* arms dealer, Chaandrran, convicted.

"I had to meet in Thailand because my promises to the Singapore secret service that I would not conduct sensitive assignments in Singapore anymore—even with United States Government personnel."

This was Colin's reference to the arms dealing conviction, arising from a "sham" arms deal in cooperation with Israel and the American government.[35]

Mak goes further to offer me to meet his CIA case officer, to see me at the Pentagon and, finally, he begins his response to the MWL cease-and-desist letter, threatening Michael Lee with his expanded powers under the Patriot Act, calling himself a protected witness by the U.S. Government.

"My partner Tony Thille and I have the USAF/Pentagon as our clients for our consulting projects hence our duty to inform them of Syrian mischief."[36]

Colin claimed he was on an S-visa to testify against the Syrian representative in a U.S. Federal court. (The United States grants S-visas to individuals who possess critical and reliable information concerning criminal or terrorist organizations.)

Colin talked a good game so I wasn't sure how much of what he said was truth. What he failed to understand was that guilty or innocent, true or false, none of his explanations would change my overriding feeling that I never wanted to hear from him again.

Losing Face

Once Colin learned that I had a "fiancé," he began to multiply and become violent for the first time, even the only persona by which I had ever known him, "warbird5k." After January 2007, new, often threatening avatars appeared in my Inbox. I was quickly learning that Michael had sorely underestimated Colin's ability to turn our lives upside down. He seemed to move effortlessly from creepy to scary. I didn't know it then, but Colin was facile in socially engineering (conning) people into trusting him, then betraying that trust by terrorizing them. His tactics were new to me, but he had been using them for years.

MWL had insulted Colin in front of me with the result of Colin's losing face, an unpardonable sin in his Singaporean culture. Over the years, Colin would often boast of his background and culture's supremacy, from its strong economy to its superior morality. A cornerstone of that culture was, and is, to maintain face and honor. The business etiquette web site, kwintessential.co.uk, provides the following bullet points on Singapore Society and Culture under the heading *Face & Respect:*

- Having face indicates personal dignity.

- Singaporeans are very sensitive to retaining face in all aspects of their lives.

- Face is a prized commodity that can be given, lost, taken away, or earned.

- It is a mark of personal qualities such as a good name, good character, and being held in esteem by one's peers.

- It can also be greater than the person and extend to family, school, company, and even the nation itself.

- Face is what makes Singaporeans strive for harmonious relationships.

Like his countrymen, Colin Mak was obsessed with saving face. He perceived my so-called rejection of him—ironically, a man whom I have never seen--as my greatest insult and repeatedly demanded apologies from me. He convinced me that the results of not complying would be horrific.

Michael's inexcusable act of causing Colin to lose of face, especially in front of his love interest (me) justified any response, up to and including bodily harm, mayhem, and murder.

Colin's preoccupation with "face" and with extorting apologies from those who had "humiliated" him would be a running theme in the thousands of emails, voicemails, defamatory blogs and sexually abusive chat sessions I was about to experience.

A Dangerous Enemy

Colin's excessive reaction to Mike was, in part the result of a combination of combustible feelings and delusions about the "relationship" between him and I. He saw Lee's email as a gauntlet, providing the opportunity to show his superiority on a virtual battlefield. Colin considered himself a "warbird," and endlessly prattled on about his military background and contacts, as well as his supposed secret training missions, even though his stint in the Singapore military was as a payroll clerk. On the other hand, at the time of the cease and desist, Colin was already a convicted arms dealer, so it was impossible to disregard his ranting completely. The man was dangerous.

In contrast, Michael's bravado was a remnant from the stage spilling over into real life. In declaring me his fiancé, Mike was probably just carried away by the moment, not a great stretch for an opera singer, whose career defines the notion of melodrama. I'm certain, however, that he never bet on the moment expanding into years of pain for the both of us.

In February, 2007, Colin sent this ominous email to Mike:

From: Colin Mai colinmai
Date: February 17, 2007 1:43:14 PM PST
To: mikelee70
Cc: leandraramm

Mike Lee
you son of a bitch
I swear to the God of Israel--
you will pay in legal and physical terms for your crimes.

In spring of 2007, under a slightly different identity, Colin (warbird) wrote Lee, and copied me, another of his tactics. He liked an audience.[37] This example, which we sent to the FBI, typifies one of many similar emails Colin would send, all of which I've kept as evidence in my case.

I will see you in summer at your f**king opera performance.
there I guarantee Federal officials and I will use nightsticks against your
f**king face
also please be informed-- you are already being investigated by the Feds.
I believe in extra-judicial methods to deal with a mother goat f**ker like you.
I guarantee you-- your family will end up poor because of you.
I CURSE YOU AND YOUR FAMILY AND YOUR RELATIONSHIPS WITH DEATH,
PAIN, CONFUSION AND DISEASE
you balless f**ker Michael you challenged me to a fight and now you back
out.
your dad must have been f**king dogs to produce an overweight singer like
you.[38]

The emails to Mike just worsened over time, cursing him "to death,"[39] threatening mutilation, disfigurement, and an end to his career if he did not apologize for unspecified wrongdoings against Colin.

Even after Michael and I were finished romantically, Colin continued to batter him with emails, making very sure that I received copies. Colin clearly basked in his superiority over my "fiancé," reducing him to virtual rubble in the process.

Although our breakup about a year later was predictably theatrical, complete with infidelity and betrayal, I tried to protect Michael from Colin's attacks. Even as late as 2010, when I finally broke free, I felt responsible for the misery Colin inflicted on Lee and thought I could ameliorate it.

A Tattered Career

Colin sent my employers and me many threatening emails, contacting every opera company I worked with at the time, including the "Martina Arroyo Foundation, Toledo Opera , Opera Carolina, Arizona Opera, New Jersey Opera Theater, Center for Contemporary Opera, St. Petersburg Opera Company, Chelsea Opera, Toledo Choral Society, Media Theatre, International Gilbert & Sullivan Festival, and Diablo Light Opera Company. Most of these opera companies said I was a liability because of the stalking and therefore could not hire me back to work."[40]

Until late summer of 2007, I ceased communications with Colin, as advised by the NYPD and FBI. Colin would taper off the communications if I showed no interest, they said, even in the face of his escalation and proliferation. Colin easily discovered where I would be performing, taunting me with all the knowledge he accumulated. The Toledo Opera had policemen outside my performances.

I had to have a strategy in place so that all of my work wouldn't dry up because I had a cyberstalker.

I decided not to make the error of being upfront about my attacker, as I had done with New Jersey Opera Theater. Their reaction to my plight was outrageous, considering that they had put Colin in touch with me to begin with. After consulting with legal counsel, that company told me in no uncertain terms that I had better control Colin and take care of it. Today, I realize what an injustice this was. As my employer, New Jersey Opera had the duty to protect me. As an employer who, without any proper vetting procedure, placed me in danger— they had negligently, if not recklessly, placed me, an employee, at great risk and then said it was all my problem and that I'd better fix it right away!

I had to figure out a way to stay one step ahead of Colin, without alarming the companies for whom I auditioned. My approach, generally, was to keep mum on the subject of Colin unless I had reason to believe he had already been in touch with that company. Then I sent out damage control emails, apologizing for Colin's communication, and downplaying his danger, even though I felt afraid most of the time.

From:leandraramm
Sent: Saturday, May 05, 2007 2:41 PM
To: Leandraramm
Cc: Leandraramm
Subject: Alert about harassing individual

To companies I have and will be working for,

I have recently become aware that Colin Mak, a man from Singapore who has been harassing me personally for months since seeing me on television in November 2005, has been maliciously contacting companies I have and will be working for.

I am reaching out to inform you that if you have received an email like this, from an address such as spicekits130 or warbird5k, there is no cause for worry according to the authorities we have contacted. I apologize if you have received any of his persistent attacks, and I ask that you please disregard his correspondence. I have never met this man and have no relationship with him.

I am in the process of taking what legal action I can to stop these disturbing attempts to affect my life and career. If you have received an email from him, I would greatly appreciate if you would let me know as it will strengthen my case against him.

I am very sorry for any trouble, and thank you for your patience and understanding.

Warm regards,

Leandra
Leandra Ramm
mezzo-soprano
www.LeandraRamm.com

Opera's Dirty Little Secrets

The prevailing treatment of me as a *persona non grata* in my time of need is, I think, a reflection of the B, C and D-level opera world attitude and culture. The layperson generally thinks of opera as this lofty art form, its management kowtowing to the whims of divas, paying them bountifully. This perception might hold true for the crème de la crème of opera, such as New York's Metropolitan Opera , or La Scala, but it is very different in the lower echelon opera companies.

The smaller establishments participate in what I call opera's "dirty little secret," a seemingly never-ending financial gouging of the talent they "nurture." For example, an audition in the smaller companies costs the auditioner money—around $50 per audition, which doesn't include accompanists. That is quite a profitable enterprise for the companies when you consider the hunger of performers for roles and the ensuing turnout by those desperate to be discovered.

Hand-in-hand with those questionable costs is the pressure music schools put on their students to remain enrolled (at a substantial fee) and get various questionable "degrees," which cost the same as a bachelor's degree but without the accreditation. By the time one receives all these degrees, she is around 30 years old, a little late in the game for high aspirations in the finer houses. Like me, many have huge student loan obligations awaiting them after their schooling. Also *de rigueur* are the outreach programs, where exhausted performers traveling by bus, must not only perform, but act as stagehands for no compensation and without proper training. This culture has little to do with singing and everything to do with saving a dollar.

Simply put, most companies regarded me and other hopefuls as an income stream. Having a stalker negatively affected that stream.

The "blame the victim" mentality was not peculiar to opera. I would experience it from the press, from law enforcement, and from prospective employers. I felt ashamed of my abuse and tried hard, albeit unsuccessfully, to keep it a secret.

Employers Don't Fail Me Now! (But They Did)

There were a handful of companies and individuals who were supportive of my stalking plight. Jim Schaeffer of Long Leaf Opera , then artistic director for Center of Contemporary Opera, was one such brave soul. He backed me and kept hiring me, despite Colin's imminent attacks on my character and the threats he would make against other performers, productions, and opera companies because of me.

Posing as Jasmine Carerra a/k/a jassbrahmos, Colin contacted Jim during the first of his major stalking period, writing:

From: "Jasmine Carerra"
Date: June 25, 2007 2:41:40 PM EDT
To: js
Subject: hi Shaeffer

I don't usually recommend beatings for cheating of 10 000 US dollars.
but this is a case of grand wire fraud.
your choice Mr Sheaffer.
you have a criminal at hand.
extra judicial methods do work.... this is not a case of harassment-- it is a case of justice.
warn Leandra-- a signed letter of apology and return of ALL monies is needed to end this.
Her parents can also look forward to a visit from me in NYC and it will not be pleasant.[41]

Jim forwarded the email to me, writing:

Dear Leandra,

...This and another email from your deranged individual arrived. At the same time, he called and identified himself as a "federal agent" wanting to know about your fraudulent activities. I told him that I knew who he was and to leave you alone. He then hung up.

I will be happy to do whatever I can do and am so sorry that you are having to go through this.

Best wishes,
Jim[42]

Jim and Long Leaf Opera were the exceptions to the rule. Most of the opera companies with whom I worked took the "blame the victim" position, judging me for having a stalker and treating me like a pariah in the industry.

The biggest offenders were the New Jersey Opera and the New York Theater Barn. I distinctly recall an audition in 2007. The moment I walked into the room, artistic director Scott Altman said something like, "You need to take care of that stalker situation." I responded that I had tried everything I could. He countered that it was "still a problem" despite their staff attorney's advice to just ignore it.

I then asked Scott if having this stalker would negatively affect my career and he responded, "Well, it could. You should email everyone you have worked with and tell them about the situation." Who was he to tell me how to handle this? New Jersey Opera Theater had lulled me into a false sense of security about Colin; they were my link to him.

Looking back, I can honestly say that the combination of Colin and the opera companies' attitude effectively squelched my opera career. Ironically, had I been a famous diva with a stalker, things would have been very different. The companies would have protected me, alerted the authorities, and contacted the media. Instead, as "the girl with the stalker" I was a liability, whom no one wanted. Simply put, the risks outweighed the rewards.

As a result, I would relocate into musical theater. It was far better to be unknown and try to begin again. The experience with NJOT taught me a valuable lesson—that not all publicity was good. I was determined to keep Colin out of my life and hide his existence from any future employers.

PART FOUR
THE TWISTED MIND OF COLIN MAK

Madman-Conman Dichotomy

At the beginning, when I wanted to believe that I had a benefactor, I thought of Colin as quirky and eccentric, characteristics that were not uncommon in the world of performing arts. After his various machinations in the Austria debacle, however, I saw him as a calculating deceiver whose agenda was dishonest. What I learned about him in the news compounded this impression—he was, after all, a convicted arms dealer.

Despite his cleverness, I was beginning to realize that he was clearly not right, suffering from paranoid delusions about our relationship, his various covert government jobs, and his top-secret work in exotic locations, like the Seychelles.[43]

His fantasies along with an alarming increase in threats of bodily harm showed a very uncontrolled, sick individual, something Colin himself recognized in one of a series of blogs published in 2008, using the moniker Colin Fritz Tan (g).

Colin's most loyal friend, Mona Hanson, whose apartment he shared in Hong Kong, had been concerned about Colin's mental state. She wrote about reconnecting with Colin after his arms dealing conviction, how he had been on good behavior, but soon after:

...the real Colin showed up again, back came the clear signs of instability: threatening emails, sexually deviant communication and emails, etc, when you didn't get what you perceived you wanted.[44]

Hanson was alarmed about Colin's stalking of various women on the Internet and called his behavior "disturbing."

In one email, she spoke of Colin's counseling session with a female psychiatrist friend, a "last ditch effort"[45] to pull him out of his downward spiral into madness.

I brought in my friend, the psychiatrist, to help you to see all the things that you were doing that was extremely unhealthy and destructive but while you listened to her, you didn't hear her and went about your life as you normally did and did not heed her advice.[46]

Kicked Around Some

Why was Colin so disturbed and violent? I think it had less to do with the military than Colin's own abusive childhood, which he talked about during one of our "at bay" Internet chats. He began by discussing my family, as he often did, fantasizing about coming to New York and asking whether he would see them—including my sister Courtney and Logan, my brother with autism. I was very protective of my family, and suggested that he stop emailing them so much—it didn't help matters. I gingerly tried to explain to him that less was more, a concept Colin, who thrived on hyperbole and excess, seemed unable to grasp.

But this chat differed slightly because Colin, for once, seemed to let down his guard, giving me a glimpse to what might underlie some of his distorted notions and behavior.

Using his original moniker, warbird5k, Colin spoke of his sister—I didn't know he had one—and about his childhood:

warbird5k: -shall I tell you a secret?
yesterday I think I saw my sister
walking just 2 meters from me and past me just outside ION shopping mall
but I cannot be sure
she was in designer clothing and carrying an expensive leather bag but I didn't make an effort to call her

me: why not?

warbird5k: or she would tell my family that I have long forgotten I have been back for some time now
I don't want my family anymore Leandra. Church friends etc have told me they are harmful to me etc
spiritually and verbally
I am better off without them
I promised my late Aunt that I would prosper very much in the USA

me: why, they are your family
family is family
no matter what
don't you think

84

warbird5k: Silvestra
sorry there was a hang
okay I was brought up speaking Hainanese-- a Chinese dialect by a very loving
foster family from young till I was about 3 or 4
Till today I still stay in touch with them
they were horrified at the abuses hurled me when they returned me to my
real family and wanted me back
I had enough of my mom and dad when I returned to Singapore after
university studies and work
they never did change
and before I left for HK and Indonesia-- they wanted 50 percent of what I
earned they said to cover their own expenses etc
I need a clean break from such abusive people
and I think till to date I made the correct decision
they contacted my visa lawyer etc and even phone my church management
and close friends

me: what kind of abuse?

warbird5k: but they all kept silent
beatings at 3
made to stand in the cold when I could not sleep etc

me: by your real parents?

warbird5k: yes
when I was older I lived with my late aunt in her home
she did show me a lot of love
I felt confused when I was younger
you cannot believe what was said in my house... [47]

If true, what Colin revealed about his childhood could explain a lot about when things began to go terribly wrong in his life. Abuse begets abuse, after all, especially when it begins at so young an age. Although his revelation didn't excuse his actions, there was a small place inside of me that it satisfied--the "why" behind his violence.

On the other hand, Colin's abuse toward me had hardened my heart and caused me to be suspicious of every word he uttered. I couldn't help but think that his childhood trauma, was, like just about everything else he wrote, a practiced, socially engineered lie, geared toward garnering my sympathy.

Method to Madness

A line from Hamlet comes to mind when I think of Colin, "Though this be madness, yet there is method in't."[48]

Like Hamlet, Colin appeared to be going, if not already, mad. He was usually on a destructive rant and his arguments rarely held up, logically. As one of his personas, Fritz Tan, he insisted he was insane, that he despised women, and that because of this, he would hurt women.[49]

Notwithstanding his impending or current psychological condition, many of Colin's attributes were that of a con artist—gaining trust through deception, using diversionary tactics, and preying on his particular mark's vulnerabilities, be they vanity, greed, or naiveté—all of which he had practiced for years on unsuspecting victims.

I have no doubt that Colin was and is psychologically disturbed.

A private investigator, hired by a Singaporean investigative firm, told me he believed Colin's problems began when he served in the Singapore military. Affirming that conclusion was Colin's outrageous behavior at Harvard and Oberlin, which happened after he entered the Singapore military. On the other hand, Colin's own chat with me showed another possibility—that Colin's beatings at age three and torture, like being made to stand out in the cold were the seed to his own depravity.

Still, Colin was a master controller and fit the profile of sociopath—a con artist who often exhibits criminal and violent traits, with a pervasive disregard for the law and the rights of others. Irrespective of his craziness, Mak was indisputably intelligent, methodical, and efficient, using time-tested modes in his stalking pursuits. Add to this his facility with all things electronic made him lethal and successful in evading capture.

Against a mastermind like Colin, law enforcement didn't stand a chance.

Cyberstalker Traits

Since he saw me on *Anderson Cooper*, Colin Mak has been as consistent a presence in my life as the sun rising in the morning. I've received over 5,000 emails, most of which are copied to myriad other friends, acquaintances, even strangers in my life. Each who received a Colin email had a purpose in my stalker's scheme. Colin was oblivious to the pain that these caused any recipient, or, more likely, relished it because then I, too, would suffer.

No one, seeing a Colin subject line, like "Bolt cutters," is immune from its toxicity. In addition to email, my stalker enjoyed blogging terabytes of defamatory data about me, the gist of which was that I'm a thieving whore without any talent. He extorted peace for a short while anyway.

But how does Colin compare to other cyberstalkers?

After doing my own research, I found a list of traits applicable to an Internet stalker and decided to see if Colin fit these criteria. Generally, a cyberstalker:[50]

- lives in a one-room apartment that hasn't been cleaned for months—if ever
- has stacks of pornographic magazines in his bedroom area, has poor personal hygiene
- has poor table manners
- has poor social etiquette
- hasn't changed the sheets on his bed for months
- has a filthy bathroom
- lives on takeout, the remnants of which litter his apartment
- may have an unusual pet (e.g., ferret) which has free run of the apartment
- is either significantly over- or underweight
- has a small moustache or other facial hair

- has not held down any job for more than a couple of years, probably less
- has no friends
- has no life outside the Internet

Since I never met Colin, I can't speak to whether he fit most of the environmental criteria listed above, like state of his bathroom, table manners, or personal hygiene.

--Living Quarters

According to his erstwhile friend Mona Hanson, Colin indeed fit some of these characteristics. Colin slept on the floor of her cramped Hong Kong apartment sometime after his arms conviction.[51] While in Singapore, he lived either at home with his mother or more recently as a transient in youth hostels.

--Pets

Although he didn't have a pet, Colin was fascinated with animal torture and my cat, Brickles.

He sent me several emails about dogs in distress, like a puppy dying after being dragged from a truck, a Labrador who leapt from a parking garage railing 80 feet above the pavement,[52] still another about a puppy thrown off a third-floor balcony, euthanized as a result.[53] He found it amusing. I was horrified.

On a more personal level, Colin focused on Brickles, in whom he took an inordinate amount of interest, even though he consistently misspelled his name. More than once, he asked me to send pictures of my cat:

SEND ME A PIC OF BIRKLES....
please
I want to see him
I love pets

He even offered to send cat food from Singapore (along with "sexy wedge heels" for me).[54] Another time he suggested:

"get your parents to take a digital photo of your cat-- just tell your parents that you are thinking of Birkles and want a picture.

Then email the picture to me okay?

I know this seems like a longwinded way to solve this little problem... but its one way I know you can make me happy... (besides a great amount of wild sex within marriage.... but lets not talk about that before I become wild.... ;).[55]

He brought up Brickles in our chat sessions, a pretty safe subject compared to my bra size—the latter being off limits. I suspected that Colin wanted Brickles' digital photograph less for sentimentality than as another means to control me. He already had access to numerous photos and videos of my family—they were online, available to anyone. He often sent these to me as attachments, hoping that I couldn't recall they'd been published, suggesting a greater familiarity with me. But we both knew he didn't have any images more personal than what was publicly available. A picture of my family pet would solve that problem and could come in handy if I "misbehaved" or "betrayed" him somehow. Well-versed in manipulating digital photographs—he admitted to pasting heads of women he stalked on porn star bodies—Colin could easily send me a doctored photo of my "dead" cat, to upset and scare me.

--Hair

No apparent facial hair on my stalker. However, he felt strongly about the hair on his head, which he impulsively shaved in 2010, then sent me photos. Many said it was an effort to conceal his identity after the arms dealing affair, but I thought it more a cry for help or evidence of his derangement.

The shaved head photos frightened me. They revealed an unbalanced individual, wearing a crazed, proud smile, reminding me of photos I'd seen of mass murderer Charles Manson after he had shaved his head in prison. If there had been any lingering doubt as to Colin's craziness, it was dispelled in those photos.[56]

--Job

Colin definitely met the cyberstalker criterion of job instability, working for several companies, just during the time I knew him. First, there was Tony Thille's Swedish company, Protec Consulting—an import-export company for military weapons, then one or two import-export companies in Hong Kong, a stint as a payroll clerk in the military, and as a sales representative for a start up online health and wellness company belonging to friend Mona Hanson. He was adept at engineering himself into jobs, not so good at keeping them.

Colin also claimed to be concurrently working for the U.S. government as a spy and as a top-secret fighter pilot—these were most likely flights of fancy from Colin's fevered but calculating imagination.

Colin's job as a photographer was real, however, in the sense that he had for years been taking pictures of young girls, leading them to believe he was "someone" in the fashion industry. He sent me many photos, including one I found particularly disturbing as the subject, a girl named Enfys was only 15, which he bragged about:

Enfys---she is a mere 15. I think I did well in this shoot as a photographer.[57]

--Friends

As far as the "no friends" prong of cyberstalker traits, I think whether Colin had friends depends on one's definition of "friends." True, he seemed to have many people at his disposal—I call these his "minions." But I seriously doubt he cared about them and am convinced his capacity for empathy was limited or non-existent.

The definition of "friend," of course, has changed since Facebook, having become its own term of art. If posting pictures of people or clicking an accept button constitutes friendship, then perhaps Colin had many of them. But in a traditional sense--as in "1. A person attached to another by feelings of affection or personal regard. ... 3. a person who is on good terms with another; a person who is not hostile"[58] —Colin was a loner.

He was anxious, however, to prove his popularity by sending me photographs, as in the following email, and providing superfluous, but exacting detail of every encounter, just to impress me. He was intent on convincing me of his legitimacy, in this case, that he legitimately had friends. In reality, these people were acquaintances he duped into socializing with him—made easier by their consumption of alcohol and his ability to act as translator.

here are pics of HK
the girl in baroque patterned dress is my new Russian friend Lena. (see www.harpianojazz.com)
she plays piano and harp for Sheraton hotel. I love her shoes. she got them in HK she tells me the two guys behind her are pilots for a russian air cargo service-- 747 jets that are too slow for my interest! ;)
we spent the night pubbing-- i drank-- but only 1 glass of wine. Lena blushes easily-- Rimma I told u got drunk!!!!
Rimma the Russian girl who speaks cantonese and mandarin was the one who took all the pics.[59]

Colin might have had many Internet friends, but these friendships were based on illusions calculated by Colin, including a goofiness and enthusiasm, which disarmed potential marks. Once he lured people into an online relationship or, in the real world, as a photographer, Colin dropped the act, displaying his unrestrained, crazy side. Any guise of friendship quickly dissipated, replaced in his new "friend" by fear and aversion.

--Sexual Deviant

The Internet stalker most likely has other unpleasant characteristics that sexual harassers possess, and the usual sexual inadequacy including lack of intimacy, controlling behavior, no concept of the partner's needs, premature ejaculation, and an abnormal belief bordering on obsession in his smallness.

Colin's obsession with his sexual inadequacy was paramount; in this way he fit the primary cyberstalker characteristic to a tee. Recognizing his perversions, of which she too would be a victim, Mak's former friend and minion Mona Hanson convinced him to see a psychiatrist in Hong Kong, where he had fled from Singapore authorities. The session, which he boasted about in the blogosphere, was an abject failure.

Colin fritz tan / 2008-07-30 15:12:27
This is Colin Fritz Tang again.[60] I am the one who is rather sick in the head, sick in mind with a very sickly and pathetic body. I am weak and just cannot get women in the right sort of way hence I have to resort to his sickly and disturbing behaviour. All you folks out there please note that I am mentally unstable and sick and should be spat and shat on.

Colin fritz tan / 2008-07-30 13:05:13
Hello everyone. I am the one and only COLIN FRITIZ(sic) TANG. I have been having some serious mental problems and have also been in care of a shrink.[61] Even my shrink has thrown me out of her clinic calling me mentally unstable and sick. I hate women of all types and take pleasure in ruining their lives. I also confirm that I link their web blogs and pictures to various porn sites. I am one of the sickest pretender out there. I cannot shoot a photo to save my life. I am a pathetic ugly son-of-a-bitch who just cannot help himself. So ladies...if you cannot forgive me...definitely do not deal with me.

Unfortunately, I had become all too familiar with Colin, the deviant.

I have sexual thoughts of you every night. Often I cannot resist it anymore and yes I do masturbate thinking of you doing it to me in every position possible.
Thinking of you screaming in pleasure.

I know you have a green brassiere-- because its in one of your photos...
partially sticking out.
nothing to be embarrassed about.[62]

During "at bay," Colin and I had regular Internet messaging chats, the prospect of which knotted my stomach because of his imminent sexual approaches.

It was difficult to sleep last night as I kept thinking of you.
Erotic thoughts.
I want us to discuss this when we chat next on google chat. Okay?[63]

I had instituted the chat sessions as a means of controlling content, diverting him from sex, threatening to sign off if he was inappropriate. I chose the lesser of two evils. The more I chatted, the less likely he'd send me email smut. During the last several months of our consensual communications, I was losing faith in that formula.

I need your intimates worn with your sweat and grime stained on them... and I need your scent.
Really! Why else would I want them if they are freshly laundered? This is getting sexual because it is...! And when I meet you I am giving you your La Senzas.... ;) [64]

Unfortunately, after cutting communications with him entirely, I confirmed that the formula's converse remained true—the less contact, the more graphic filth I'd receive.

The Colin Blueprint

The upside, if you could call it that, to the volume of his emails, was the patterns they uncovered, Colin's unique calling card of traits and tactics. The most prevalent was his assumption of multiple identities, which allowed him to simultaneously harass and stalk from many different vantage points, while hiding in plain sight.

--Impersonation

"All the world's a stage,
And all the men and women merely players:
They have their exits and their entrances;
And one man in his time plays many parts..."
—William Shakespeare, *As You Like It*, 1600

I was raised to own my identity, one reason why I never went underground in my fight against Colin. My mother, sister, and I were performers—our identity was our brand. I lived a transparent life, as did my family—we had nothing to hide.

On the other hand, as an actress, I was a professional impostor, playing roles to convince an audience.

Ironically, Colin, the amateur impostor, had fooled me, the trained performer. Clearly, I was the amateur in his concocted universe. Online, he was very convincing and bragged about having several Facebook personas. Curious, I found stormorochalie, Colin Mak and, of course, his standby, warbird5k. For all I knew, there were dozens, maybe hundreds more.

In one of our forced Internet chat sessions, Colin described piecing together a Facebook Frankenstein monster using the head of an unknown woman and my address. His sole purpose as usual was manipulation—in this case to convince a newly garnered Swiss "friend" to deliver a package to me.

Below, Colin is "warbird5k," calling me Silvestra, an operatic role I had played years previously to critical acclaim. Even chatting in real time, Colin preferred metaphors and fantasy to real talk, jealously guarding who he really was, or, worse, not knowing the difference.

warbird5k: the facebook profile said I was from Switz but working in NYC"

me: who's picture did you use?"

warbird5k: I don't even know, it was a woman who had dark hair late 30s random on the internet"

me: did you give my name with the address?

warbird5k: no
just said send to Silvestra with your address
never gave last name

me: please be more careful in the future with my address!

warbird5k: Silvestra c/o Jasmine okay I will baby"[65]

I exhorted Colin not to give out my personal address—ever—and admonished him for impersonating people, creating fake profiles. He disagreed with the term "fake profile"—for him it was a real profile, and a real account. More evidence that Colin himself couldn't distinguish between fact and fiction.

In his duping of the Swiss Facebook friend, Colin posed as a female, Jasmine, a persona I associated with some of his most ruthless emails to me.

warbird5k: no it was another Facebook account besides my regular one
I wanted to experiment to see how far some stupid internet people would go to send gifts to "Jasmine."
I hate facebook
full of weird people

me: ok
just don't do it again

warbird5k: I can show you that fake account
okay I promise[66]

Colin stalked me by using hundreds of email personas, often changing the extension of the email (e.g., yahoo.com; gmail.com) or capitalization (e.g., MIGGY MIGGY vs. miggy!).[67] At first, I thought he was working in concert with others; I had heard that cyberstalkers often work in pairs. But quickly I realized that they were all Colin, that the variety of addresses was just a mode of obfuscation and there were unlimited creatable email addresses.

As a rule, Colin had taught me extreme reservation when it came to any Internet correspondence, even from people I knew. I'd learned to avoid the obvious--emails from warbird, miggy, stormorochalie, jazz brahmos, or any variation of those. Still, my career depended on outreach to new business contacts and their outreach to me, so I was vulnerable to unfamiliar emails whose attributes seemed credible. My curiosity and fear of losing a potential deal would cause me to open mail with bated breath. Curiosity was one of Colin's most reliable allies.

Getting me to open emails was one way of controlling me. Impersonating me in emails to my friends and colleagues was another. In one especially damaging instance, Mak, pretending to be me, sent an email to my management company, instructing it to remove me from its client roster. I only learned about this after a visit to the management Web site, which showed no trace of me anywhere. When I called them, questioning why I was no longer listed, they were puzzled—hadn't I just instructed them to end our relationship?

I felt powerless against Colin, whose lies even long-standing business associates trusted more than they did my own   true   words.

--The Importance of Gene Pools—Repository Genes

Colin held his Chinese genetics in great reverence, constantly claiming superiority over other backgrounds. Although he prided himself on learning many languages and dialects, the Chinese and Singapore ways were superior.

In short, Colin was a xenophobe.

darling Leandra

I have learnt some things from my travels--

I am very blessed to be able to speak many languages-- including the Chinese dialect Cantonese which is widely used in China and Hong Kong. I speak Mandarin well-- therefore I get special prices etc at shops.

speaking German, Russian etc-- helps make these Western people comfortable... I have made a lot of friends that way...

well one thing to live a successful life I have learnt-- is to get along well with people.[68]

Colin often used his Chinese roots and connections to threaten people, in this case Michael Wade Lee, who at the time of the following email, was slated to sing the lead in Madama Butterfly in Hong Kong. Colin poses here as "April Mendez":

April Mendez <veritas30>
your Hong Kong performance of Madama Butterfly-- Very Important.
October 23, 2008 3:41 AM

Michael Wade Lee,
You must make arrangements to turn back from HK and not perform as Navy Lt Pinkerton.

I know that the rank of Lt in the Navy is equivalent to Colonel in the other branches of the armed forces but in this case the rank bestowed on you is only operatic and amounts to nothing.

Its because I know people in the 2nd Directorate of the People's Liberation Army... (I have spent roughly a year in the HK and the PLA building is at the former Ritz Carlton Hotel)... the PLA's intelligence department, who will not be pleased that you will enter HK... we can make arrangements to deport you at immigration or get you at the Green Room of your opera site-- most likely the Cultural Center in Tsim Sha Shui. Its up to you.

I am ethnic Chinese and we Chinese protect our own. I speak and write fluent Chinese and Cantonese -- and I think you will not want to learn these two languages via the express route with the PLA and the Public Security Bureau . China and Greater China are lands in which you will not understand either the culture, norms or language.

Please take my advice and cancel any and all arrangements for Asia. Asia will not welcome you and this expedition could prove to be detrimental.[69]

Leave Leandra alone.

--Repository Genes

I'd long suspected that my gene pool held a huge fascination for Colin, and was an essential element in why he chose to pursue me over other victims.

He confirmed my suspicion later, writing:

You know my standards... I asked God for a girl made in a petri dish and I will have her at all costs!![70]

... and sending me articles about test-tube baby pioneer Robert Edwards winning the 2010 Nobel Prize in medicine.[71]

My genius gene pool complemented Colin's obsession with "untermenschen" and other genetic undesirables, although he began to doubt my superiority.

Leandra
may I take a look at the medical report of DONOR CLEAR?
I am curious... I can interpret that report with my bio training...
can you?[72]

In the end, Colin used my genius sperm bank genetics against me, depicting it as a vulnerability rather than an asset. He enjoyed dangling my "failures" before me, made all the more unforgivable because my genes foretold something better. Many successful opera singers and musicians came from undistinguished genetic backgrounds. Shouldn't I, who had a leg up genetically, be outshining the lot of them? Naturally, he never would acknowledge or even recognize his role in cutting short any leverage I'd previously gained in my career.

Colin relished instilling doubt about the gene pool's efficacy, writing my parents about Doron Blake, who appeared as a baby on *Phil Donahue*, and whom Colin later saw as an adult.

"DORON BLAKE looks like a moron and speaking ant head in the Genius Sperm Bank movie
ask him to get a shave please..."[73]

Colin targeted my autistic brother Logan, also a product of the Genius Sperm Bank, as another illustrative failure.

"You are a loser and your family is also a family of losers.. why David Plotz did not state the singular failure and loser of the Genius Sperm Bank-- LOGAN RAMM is autistic..";[74]
"please tell your f**king autistic brother-- I wonder who will marry him. what is his IQ since he is autistic? Was the Genius Sperm Bank created to create people of his species?
f**k him. he is the RUNT of the Ramm family.;[75]
Fwd: Autism-- Logan might as well end his life-- he is a genius sperm bank alum but yet socially inept. FU*k you Ramm family. Leandra you are now known as Leandra Fat C**t RamM!@!"[76]

--National Pride

Colin prided himself in his classical fascist characteristics—nationalistic, and unyielding with an idolatry of the state superseding all else.

"today is my country's very own 45th National Day and we are celebrating it on a high note—world economic growth in all percentages, surpassing the US, India, China, Brazil and in spite of difficulties in 2008-2009, high employment and a vibrant economy. I am proud of my country's achievements though I have lived for long period in US, Europe and Hong Kong...There is no place like home where there is almost zero crime and corruption."

He often sent me articles demonstrating the superiority of Singapore over the United States, lauding its economic growth:[77]

"What do you have in New York? A rich socialite who has invited you to sing on her yacht? You must be at a loss as to what to do now Leandra—Goldman Sachs just took a hit yesterday with its earnings release.

It will cascade down to every sector in New York that means you included. I foresee a banker becoming a waitress in your restaurant....Contrast this to Singapore—we have had WORLD RECORD BREAKING Economic growth...surpassing even the BRICs—Brazil, Russian India and China. WE have 25 percent growth!!! See below!"[78] and cultural attributes.

"The government in Singapore values artists—both foreign and local more than the US government does.", [79]"In short Singapore had much more problems than America ever had as a nation state! We have achieved racial and religious harmony which I believe is still not totally present in the US. I am glad Raffles saw in his heart and mind what Singapore would be! He was the one Anglogphone that I respect!"[80]

How ironic that an inveterate criminal stalker with his base of operations in Singapore should laud the lack of crime there. Extolling racial equality was equally contradictory, given his omnipresent racism.

--Untermenschen and Undesirables[81]

A corollary to Colin's national pride (both Singaporean and Chinese), was his distaste for certain racial and ethnic groups. It's not surprising that he often used Hitler's term "untermenschen" in his emails and in his Internet chat sessions, as he did in August 2009, below:

Warbird5k: u know what untermenchen is yes?

me: no

warbird5k: what????
its German for sub-human[82]

Colin used his hate tactic to bolster his own self-image—employing classical misdirection techniques of a conman, with the fervor of an unapologetic racist. Aside from Singapore nationals and Chinese, no group was exempt from his superfluous bigoted comments like, "that's why I despise Thais so much,"[83] or excoriating the Ukrainians:

"I understand you are a product of Ukraine—and I know your history having studies its language for a time. You are part of the product o history from the [Cyrillic term] in which 27 million people died, hurts remain and certain non-Western business practices do happened even after post-war years. Regrettably."[84]

Colin detested homosexuals, too, whom he considered "sexual deviants," evident in the following email, posing as "Frank Tobias." Colin attacks a Singapore stylist, Darin, a "South "African gay guy":[85]

Darin
you sick gay male prostitute and pervert. (as if I don't know you aren't gay)
my girlfriend has told me you wrote about me using my name on a blog
I shall be going to your shop soon with a nightstick to beat you up in HK.
you can be sure the nightstick will be seared over a bunsen burner then used to cauterize your ass. That will put a stop to your sexual deviancy.[86]

He reveals his racism, even in his self-perceived largesse toward certain people. Below, he assures proprietor Ana Liew, a Singapore boutique owner whom he extorted, that he will "call off strikes" against her assistant, Jeannette, because she is a Filipina:

I have given my word to Jeannette that she will not be harmed—because I do have a special affection for Filipinos in my church that I will adhere to the agreement signed.[87]

Stereotyping racial traits fit in nicely with Colin's technique of peppering his lies with grains of truth.

--Lies Peppered with Truth: Divas Gone Wild

Colin was a pro at manipulating the truth—maybe taking a half a percent of truth, or use a real name, and everything else false—creating a new version of the truth, the one published on the Web. A distortion of the Cartesian, *"Cogito ergo sum,"*[88] simply by virtue of its existence, something posted online gives it authenticity. By the time he found me, Mak was experienced at blogging, ensuring that his version of reality reached untold numbers of people who might search for me.

Colin constructed various defamatory blogs about me, the most notorious being "Divas Gone Wild," published in 2011. He described me as an "undercover prostitute" with several cast members, including Tim Hill, my former colleague from Toledo, "charging as much or as little as 25 US Dollars for a blowjob," accusing me of defrauding "someone from Hong Kong of 10,000 USD for David Ramm's heart operation ...," falsifying identities, such as Maureen Fitzgerald, claiming, "You owe us a lot of money and many people apologies after hurting them and sexually harassing them and threatening them with police reports if they don't do your bidding."[89]

Colin was particularly fond of using my own ideas against me. He was successful, for example, in bringing copyright infringement suits under the Digital Millennium Copyright Act against me, resulting in Google's Blogger and YouTube demanding removal of material from my sites. In the meantime, he defamed me all over the Internet, especially in his final stalking phase, beginning in spring 2010 until his arrest. Reporting to Blogger about Mak's defamatory blogs garnered the following response:

"Blogger does not remove allegedly defamatory, libelous, or slanderous material from Blogger.com or Blogspot.com. If a contact email address is listed on the blog, we recommend you working directly with the author to have the content in question removed or changed."[90]

--Affronts and Apologies

As part of his humiliation and extortion tactics, Mak demanded apologies for some vaguely formulated affront, as in this email, early in his first elevated stalking period.

From: Colin MaK <warbird5k>
Subject: 24 hours
Date: January 27, 2007 6:18:54 AM PST
To: mikelee70
Cc: Leandra Erin Ramm leandraramm

Mr Michael Wade Lee,

The Time now is 9am EST 27th Jan 2007.

You have 24 hours to write me a letter of apology via email or I am telling my CIA case officer about your threats--- I notice you did not CC Leandra Ramm in your most threatening letter(s) to me previously.
I want to be your friend, not your legal opponent.
Thank you in advance for your cooperation.

And later:

Mike
I CURSE YOUR FAMILY WITH OVERWHELMING PAINFUL CANCERS AND DISEASE FOR YOUR UNGRATEFULNESS.
F**K YOU. YOU SHOULD BE GIVING ME RESPECT.
AND I STILL NEED THAT F**KING SIGNED LETTER OF APOLOGY.
IF I DO NOT RECEIVE IT-- YOU WILL KNOW WHAT HAPPENS WITH YOU.
DONT EVEN THINK OF GOING NEAR LEANDRA WHEN YOU ARE SO POOR.
SHE DOES NOT EVEN NEED YOU.[91]

There were thousands of similarly themed communications, demanding apologies from me, my family, my boyfriends, for taking money, for using another representative, for not contacting him, for humiliating him. They all boiled down to losing face, and with Colin, just about anything constituted a gauntlet thrown down.

When I finally reached out to Colin in 2007, initiating my "at bay" period, I began my phone call with an apology, although I had done nothing wrong. I learned quickly that despite his incessant demand for apologies, receiving them did not quell his stalking.

--Nightsticks and Boxcutters

My cyberterrorist preferred certain weapons to threaten bodily harm. A particular favorite was to bludgeon any or all of us with nightsticks.

Long after Michael and I had parted ways, Colin still sent threats to him, copying our mutual agent, Robert Gilder and me.

Dear Michael
I am writing to inform you that soon enough you will be bludgeoned soon enough. THIS WILL ALSO BE THE FATE OF THE BLONDE THAT ACCOMPANIED YOU TO HK.
DO NOT ATTACK SOMETHING YOU DO NOT WISH and CANNOT TO KILL MICHAEL WADE LEE YOU WHITE TRASH.
HONG KONG IS THE HOMELAND OF MY ANCESTORS AND YOU HAD NO RIGHT TO BE THERE.
THE BLUDGEONING ATTACK WILL REMOVE YOUR OPERA SINGING CAPABILITY AS WELL AS LEAVE YOU WITH SEVERAL BROKEN FACIAL AND APPENDAGE BONES.
WEAPONS USED WILL BE THE US GOVERNMENT ISSUE PR-24 NIGHTSTICKS.[92]

Colin liked box cutters, bolt cutters and knives, too, as he wrote to the same group:

"I swear to the God of Israel—you will be stabbed at least 40 times with a steak knife and your face and genitals mutilated so you will not be able to perform in operas anymore the more trouble Leandra gives me."[93]

The goal was severe bodily harm to people I knew, who were important to me.

Dustin
I am going to beat up Leandra Ramm after I blind you and cut your face with a box cutter
You asked for all this. You instigated this. You know how much I loved her and still do.
Beating of Leandra will be done in NYC just as she exits 321 Main Street to go to work.[94]

Ultimately, his fantasy was to mutilate or simply kill me.

"I will beat you up and cut up your face with a box Cutter Leandra, I swear it.[95]

PART FIVE
CONTEMPORANEOUS VICTIMS

Collateral Damage

Every time I thought I had taken proper precautionary measures with my employers, family, and friends, Colin not only continued his current stalking, but expanded his realm to more and more people. Trying to stop Colin by preemption was like plugging a burst dam with my pinky finger.

Colin seemed to relish increasing his email pool linked to me, using the ripple effect to find his next victim. He began with people closest to me, soon touching those I barely knew, but connected with me in his mind. I considered these victims collateral damage in Colin's war on me.

My Family

Colin was relentless in his attacks on my family. Adrienne shared information about us freely, never taking any precautions to obfuscate their lives. Just the opposite—my mother talked freely about our family on network television, in documentaries, to newspapers and magazines. Consequently, Colin knew where my parents and autistic brother lived, home and business phone numbers, and email addresses. He collected details about my father's health, my mother's job, and Logan.

He knew a lot more about us than we did about him.

Below is an early email, targeting all five of us, which I forwarded to David Plotz that very night. Attached to the email was an old family photograph of Adrienne, Logan, myself, Courtney, and David Ramm.

Colin Mak warbird5k
MAY THE SPIRIT OF DEATH BE UPON THE RAMM FAMILY
May 5, 2007 7:51 PM
MAY THE SPIRIT OF DEATH BE UPON THE RAMM FAMILY!
because Leandra the slut has lied to me and conspired to harm me with Michael Wade Lee--
when I have sponsored her and done favors for her etc.
May the Satan have a free hand on the Ramm family--and eliminate each one of them with heart attacks, mysterious ailments, mental distress, financial poverty, various cancers, thyroid problems
May their enemies continually seek their lives!!
F**K YOU LEANDRA-- YOU ARE A SLUT.

There were hundreds of intervening emails, some just with a subject line, like, "I will smash your f**king family to bits."[96] Or "assault on the Ramms."[97]

Mak employed his well-worn tactics of false accusations, demanding apologies, and threatening bodily harm against my family, with the added relish of attacking Michael Wade Lee.

Original Message --------
Subject: Warning to the Ramm family

Date: Fri, 01 Jun 2007 23:57:04 -0700
From: Colin M
To: rammda, leandraramm
Adrienne and David Ramm,

2 weeks ago-- I gave you a call and a warning. That was at 730am in the morning at your NY residence.
I am now in Washington DC on a confidential assignment--
I am prepared to meet you with my Federal officer escorts who already know about the incident with Michael Wade Lee.
I demand an apology from you, and Leandra Ramm about the kinds of deceptions and insults you have given me and the cash I have sent to Leandra returned.
I am also prepared to use a nightstick on you, and Leandra.
Leandra-- I do not take insults, lies and deceptions easily-- that you should know. Be a bitch and I will be a bulldog that will bite at your crotch.
however if you refuse to play by my rules-- especially when it comes to business relationships...
I will come after you.
This includes Michael Wade Lee the loser.

After ending our "at bay" arrangement, Colin became more relentless against my family, even sending a fax to my mother's workplace. The fax, sent through an online service called fax ZERO, was dated Friday, August 13, 2010, at 9:29 AM.

To: Adrienne Ramm.___. Pianist
Company: Ballet Academy East...
Sender Information
From: Colin
Company: Stormo Rochalie
Email address: SpitzerSO

Dear Adrienne Ramm
I pray this fax reaches you well.
Get your daughter Leandra Ramm to talk to me and I will not carry out the beating and blinding
of Dustin Bear the saxophonist in due time.
I forgive your daughter Leandra for what she did—but we need to talk.
I pray the time will not come when I have to confront you at Ballet East, break things, etc to ask You to ask Leandra to reprent.

Leandra is very important to me and I love her a lot. I have spend a lot of money on her...Leandra knows how to contact me—get her to talk to me on google chat.[98]

By 2011, his extortion and threats of violence were more specific. Claiming he'd be in New York the following week, he demands an apology, the absence of which would result in the following:

I would want COURNTEY RAMM your little sister to be raped and beaten and your autistic brother LOGAN RAMM to suffer the same fate. I know autistic people have very very low IQ hence his self-defence capabilities are non-existent. Courtney Ramm works at YogaWorks in NYC. I know where to find her.[99]

Attacking Logan

Colin's attacks on Logan are hate crimes and, as such, should be prosecuted under our laws. Colin picked on Logan because of his disability. I my mind, that made these attacks the least forgivable.

"I have decided that after the expiry time of 72 hours---I will go to NYC after my UK Seychelles assignment and beat up LOGAN RAMM your brother.

From the oldest to the youngest Ramm—all will be involved in your sin of betrayal...Adrienne, David, Courtney, Logan and you. Why should I not include Logan on the list because he is 'not as talented and is autistic?'...This hatred etc. all needs to end Leandra. I don't want to have to be forced to beat up or otherwise physically harm you or youngest brother Logan. He is precious to all involved considering the money and effort your parents went through to create each of you from the GSB...I know he is innocent—that is the purity and value of the sacrifice!"[100]

And,

"I have very little regard for autistic people...";[101]
are you so proud that he is autistic but also from the genius sperm bank... what the f**k is this
Leandra is autistic too given the fact she is so stupid![102]
I don't need you now Leandra--
you are nothing but a prostitute as is confirmed by several of your friends
you come from a loser family that paid much money to create Logan-- only to have created a Mongoloidal autistic.
weird weird![103]

I'm grateful that my brother doesn't have an email address and that we protected him from my stalker's hate as much as we could.

Logan knew how much Colin was disrupting our home. Most of the time my parents refused to pick up the continually ringing phone—Colin calling for hours at a time, leaving hateful voicemails, abusing and victimizing my family in their own home, a captive audience of endless answering machine messages, just waiting for it to stop.

One time, though, Logan answered the phone, taking Colin by surprise. He told Colin to leave us the f**k alone, or words to that effect. Responding typically as a bully confronted, Colin abruptly hung up the phone. For several years afterward, Colin brought up my brother's audacity in fighting back. Obviously, my disabled brother had hit a nerve.

Leading Men: Boyfriends

Colin primarily stalked women, and my case was no different. But since he thought of me as *his* woman, the idea of another man in my life drove him to elevated madness. This was the case with my two boyfriends, MWL and Dustin Bear.

Mak's ruthless attack on Lee was not solely to "get at" me. Mak considered my boyfriends the greatest threat to his imaginary romance with me. He refused to accept that I was sexually active and in another man's arms, becoming enraged at the notion, especially since Chinese culture holds virginity in such high esteem.

Because Colin could now identify a man in my life, he became relentless against MWL, accusing him of being a criminal, stealing money, threatening a federal witness, sexually harassing a soprano with whom he had performed, and contacting his employers.

In summer of 2008, MWL took the bait, responding to Colin, who had been pestering him about the nature of our relationship. Lee wrote:

From: MichaelWadeLee
Date: Thu, 7 Aug 2008 14:13:59 -0400
Subject: Re: (no subject)
To: spitzers50

Although it is none of your business what Leandra and I shared, since you say you need to know the truth, yes, absolutely, at one time, we were very serious in a romantic relationship together. That relationship is over. I have moved on. I assume she has too.

I have no contact with her anymore nor do I wish any more contact with her.

I am no longer interested in Leandra.

She is not my responsibility anymore.

If you are interested in her, pursue her. Do whatever you want. But please leave me out of it.

Now that I have told you what you want to know, please, I kindly request that you please stop contacting me.

I am letting you know that I am blocking your address after this message.

Colin, in total denial, was still asking me about Lee in 2009 and 2010:

"I do not think he was your fiancée. In fact I reckon he was just a friend-because time was too short for you to have developed anything for him."[104]

He couldn't let go, threatening me with harm if I didn't give him the answer he wanted about my relationship with MWL. Below, he addresses me as Silvestra, derived from my role in *Mario and the Magician*, in which the critic labeled me a "Sultry Silvestra."

Silvestra,
I do not like the Michael Wade Lee situation. He tried to destroy me before
Was he really your boyfriend? or fiancee?

I think it was neither. What was your nature of your relationship with him? Was it sexual as he claimed to me in the Olympic period? I still have emails from that time which I had shown you before. If you do not answer this email I assure you your punishment too is on the way. I might be angry if the answer is yes but I would be angry if you deny the truth. I don't think Michael Wade Lee was telling the truth because he was getting back at me. However how is it that in the period that we did not talk he gave phone calls to me after I called you in April 2007 and had access to your email and read it? Did you forward my email to him? Also did he write from your email account?[105]

Attempting to control the discussion, I responded to Colin:

Please give me a phone number where I can call you to discuss these matters. Please give me an exact day and time.
Silvestra[106]

Colin began attacking Michael Wade Lee in 2007 and continued well after our relationship ended. Colin enjoyed toying with Lee, telling him:

Michael
I am seeing Leandra Ramm shortly on her ship and I am given no instructions as to how to meet her etc. She was the one that caused me to spend several thousand dollars on the cruise ship tickets. She has not bothered to come

online to talk to me about the tickets yet despite my desperate pleas-- and I have spent more than you will ever earn in your opera performances.

Her family will NOT be harmed but you will be because you posed as her fiancee 3 years ago and harmed our relationship by throwing in poison in it-- thus creating suspicions and discord by giving sexual details about your imagined trysts with Leandra to spite me. You f**king lied to me to cause problems with me and Leandra.

I swear to the God of Israel-- you will be stabbed at least 40 times with a steak knife and your face and genitals mutilated so you will not be able to perform in operas anymore the more trouble Leandra gives me.

Leandra we do need to talk soon before I expand the combat theatre.

Leandra upon hearing from you I will stand down all attacks on Michael Wade Lee-- it costs me just 500 USD to get him iced in Europe where he will perform.

Pinnacle Arts/Robert Gilder-- your office will come under attack soon too if my situation with Leandra is not resolved-- because I am talking about great losses of money here on my side with the cruise ship tickets.

Leandra-- you are hurting people, albeit not yourself the more you f**k up this situation. You have already used up a great deal of goodwill with me

In the following email, subject line "Bolt cutter," he includes Lee, although his primary target was Dustin Bear, who in 2010 had revealed himself as my boyfriend to Colin.

From: MiGGY MiGGY miggymiggy90
Date: November 6, 2010 6:26:55 AM EDT
To: bearsax, bearsax, info
Cc: leandraopera, leandraramm, leandraramm, rammda, courtneyramm, Lauren Kampf laurenkampf, exodus
Subject: BOLT CUTTER

HI Dustin and Michael Wade Lee

since I might be cutting your sorry and very small off with the following tool-- a giant bolt cutter
http://www.botachtactical.com/dynenbulbol.html
would you like to buy this ahead of me-- I would prefer of you self-castrate than to dirty my hands.
Please make a youtube video

Dustin-- your mother deserves to be raped and beaten to death.

Later, Colin would send pictures of Dustin to my family and me, the only text appearing in the subject line, in about 20-point bold-faced font, **"target for rape, beatings and death"**,[107] followed ten minutes later, by the following:

"Dear all
I am planning the beating of the following person DUSTIN BEAR in the pictures here—any of you want to join in?"[108]

Co-Stars: Tim Hill—Bass-Baritone

Colin would socially engineer other men to get to me—they weren't love interests, but co-performers. One of these was Tim Hill, a bass–baritone opera singer, whom Colin discovered was performing with Toledo Opera at the same time I was working for that company.

I still haven't figured out how Colin chose some of his peripheral victims, like Tim. The goal was always to get to me, especially during his stalking episodes, as opposed to the "at bay" period, when I exerted some control over his harassment.

I suspect that he chose male victims according to their "threat level" to Colin, prospective boyfriends topping the list. Tim slightly resembled Michael Wade Lee—both were burly, handsome, and had similar coloring. Colin knew that Lee and I had been involved in a sexual relationship, although he constantly tried to cast doubt on that fact. Perhaps Hill presented a similar template to Colin—a potential lover he had to vanquish, although later Colin would post on DivasGoneWild that Tim was gay and I had forced him into sexual relations. Or maybe Tim was just a crime of opportunity—easy to access on the Internet (where his email was posted) and close in proximity to me.

The following email exchange between Colin and Tim from spring 2007 is a microcosm of Colin's technique, beginning with his flattery to gain information. Tim's eagerness in retaining a sponsor was more guarded than mine. Where I had handed Colin the keys to the kingdom with respect to my private information, Tim didn't provide his telephone number. And, luckiest for Tim, was that he wasn't the ultimate target. Colin would grow bored once he was through using him.

From: Miggy M spicekits130
Sent: Sunday, April 22, 2007 07:03 PM
To: tim
Subject: HI TIM Hill Baritone!

HI--My name is Miggy Gulnara and quite some time ago I saw your "Figaro" show. You are quite a singer and we would like to hire you for a corporate event what is your cellular number to call?

From: tim@
To: spicekits130
Date: Mon, 23 Apr 2007 04:07:35 +0000
Subject: Re: HI TIM Hill Baritone!

Hi Miggy,
Thank you for your inquiry. What date or dates are you looking for? I am currently working on a Tosca in Ohio and am out of the Tri-state area. What music are you interested in having? What number can I call you at?
Best regards,
Tim Hill

From: Miggy M spicekits130
Sent: Saturday, May 5, 2007 06:55 PM
To: 'Tim Hill'
Subject: RE: HI TIM Hill Baritone!

I am in south America now and need to arrange for a corporate event featuring your singing. What number can I get you at?

From: tim
To: spicekits130
Date: Sun, 6 May 2007 03:19:13 +0000
Subject: Re: HI TIM Hill Baritone!

Hi Miggy
Can we discuss via email? I am very busy with shows right now.
Thanks,
Tim

From: Miggy M mailto:spicekits130
To: 'Tim Hill'
Subject: RE: HI TIM Hill Baritone!

the problem is -- this part of south America I am at--is difficult to get to an Internet Cafe. Its easier to get to a phone instead. I also need to talk to you about some things about the show we have in mind-- that I prefer to speak about than to write about...>

From: tim
To: spicekits130
Date: Sun, 6 May 2007 14:47:01 +0000

Subject: Re: HI TIM Hill Baritone!

Honestly Miggy, I don't give out my cell phone to people I don't know. I have had problems in the past. I am sorry if this inconveniences you, but I have to think of my own personal well being here. Tim

From: Miggy M [mailto:spicekits130]
Sent: Saturday, May 19, 2007 11:40 AM
To: 'Tim Hill

This is not a threat but a PROMISE. Tell Leandra Ramm--- I have been kind to her... I expect reciprocation-- not deceptions, lies and ill treatment-- anything less and it will be an eye for an eye, a tooth for a tooth, skin for skin and flesh for flesh.tell her we will strike-- and the strike will be righteous, forceful, precise and even painful-- with nightsticks. I don't give a f**k that she was a test tube baby-- its only cum that made her.her mother Adrienne Ramm was warned today at 730 EST.all we need is a letter of apology from that slut Leandra-- a signed letter-- nothing less... a letter stating in no uncertain terms her lies, deceptions and withholding of information, and threats against us.

From: tim
To: spicekits130
Date: Sat, 19 May 2007 15:50:36 +0000>
Subject: Re: > >

Dear Miggy,
I don't know who you are nor what your grief with Leandra is, but I believe this is something you need to take up with her--not a work colleague.

Yes, I work with Leandra, and that is all.

I do not deliver these types of threats or promises, because I do not want to be a part of others problems.

Now, I am certainly glad I never gave you my contact information. You are to NEVER write me again.

Sincerely,
Tim Hill

From: Miggy M [mailto:spicekits130]
Sent: Saturday, May 19, 2007 12:01 PM
To: 'Tim Hill'
Subject: RE:

Dear Tim--it is something YOU need to take to her. We warned her about the consequences before and she did not respond.We used to sponsor her in the

126

past before-- but we discovered that money -- thousands of dollars was used with ingratitude.We just need you to warn her.We give Leandra just till Monday to respond... no response and we guarantee that by Tuesday-- broken bones and perforated will happen. This will happen at your rehearsal I guarantee.Tell Leandra this-- we tried Mr and Missus Nicetie previously-- but this did not work. We were trying to get what we wanted without broken crockery but she did not respond well.oh we certainly have your cellular phone as well-- we work for the US Government.all we need is a letter of apology (a signed one) thats all.

From: tim
To: spicekits130
Date: Sat, 19 May 2007 16:07:16 +0000
Subject: Re:

You are clearly a raving lunatic. If you continue to contact me and I find out who you are, I will sue you for harassment. I have no dealings with delivery of messages. If you work for the government, you know there are laws against bodily injuries at a rehearsal. You are threatening me for something that I was never involved in.

Your problems are with Leandra, not me.

I say this one final time. NEVER CONTACT ME AGAIN.

Tim Hill

From: Miggy M [mailto:spicekits130]
Sent: Saturday, May 19, 2007 12:22 PM
To: 'Tim Hill', leandraramm
Subject: RE:

I am not threatening you. Leandra knows who I am if you send her this message. if not during rehearsals thats fine. I work for a government agency-- a very powerful one I might add. Ask Leandra. ONCE AGAIN-- OUR STRIKE WILL BE VERY PAINFUL FOR LEANDRA TO BEAR.

From: tim
To: spicekits130
Date: Sat, 19 May 2007 16:27:49 +0000
Subject: Re:

I have reported you to the Abuse Center at Hotmail.

You deal with your own problems...DO NOT CONTACT ME.

I WILL SUE YOU FOR HARASSMENT IF YOU DO NOT QUIT WRITING ME.

I WILL NOT RESPOND TO ANY OTHER EMAILS FROM YOU.

Sincerely,
Tim Hill

From: Miggy M [mailto:spicekits130]
Sent: Saturday, May 19, 2007 07:34 PM
To: 'Tim Hill'
Subject: RE: OHIO

I know Ohio well. I was in Oberlin. Just because Leandra is in Toldedo and I am in New York does not mean she is beyond our strike radius. You are not my enemy either, and neither do I want Leandra to be my enemy. But things can become pretty ugly-- as they are already-- if Leandra does not restore things as they were before for the evil words she said and things she done. Look--- we are all reasonable people here-- I understand people commit sins and mistakes along the way. I am just looking for an apology, nothing more for Leandra-- I am not looking to f**k her in any way though she does have big breasts. I just need you to tell her-- injuries can and will happen if my instructions are not followed. I was her sponsor--- I have the supreme right to demand the bare minimum.

In order to rid himself of Mak, Tim felt cornered into feigning his intense dislike for me in an email to Colin, even calling me a "c**t." Tim didn't realize that encouraging Colin in writing would have quite the opposite effect, something Colin would eternally keep alive and manipulate.

Although hurtful, I entirely appreciated the desperate need to be rid of Colin. It was each man for himself.

Mike Hogan—The Full Monty

It was May 2010 on a cruise ship in the Caribbean. I had recently cut ties with Colin, who, as a result, began emailing Mike Hogan, a co-star in Media Theater's 2008 production of *The Full Monty*. As with many of my previous cast members, Mike and I remained friends and communicated on Facebook. Monitoring my every move, Colin had seen recent activity between Mike and me on that site, one of the downsides of being visible in real time.

It begins, as do all cons, with the ruse of urgency. Colin needed information about me to pass on to my parents. Right away. Mike responded:

Date: Mon, 17 May 2010 00:13:23 -0700
From: mhogan80
Subject: Re: hi MIKE HOGAN-- Leandra Ramm
To: spitzers50

Sorry. I don't have any other contact info for her other than what u have. I don't know her family. Are u worried she is in any danger?? I only talk to her on facebook.
Michael Hogan

On Mon, 5/17/10, MiGGY MIGGY miggymiggy wrote:
From: MiGGY MIGGY miggymiggy
Subject: RE: hi MIKE HOGAN-- Leandra Ramm
To: mhogan80
Date: Monday, May 17, 2010, 10:34 AM

the point is when someone sponsors you, cares for you, loves you etc you don't want to be treated shabbily as I perceive things to be now
I am on this ship and demand that she invites me to meet her.
I will pay for her friend's meals at the restaurant as well.

Date: Mon, 17 May 2010 10:16:53 -0700
From: mhogan80
Subject: RE: hi MIKE HOGAN-- Leandra Ramm
To: spitzers50
This is a very bizarre (sic) request. You want me to call her parents so they can call her and tell her to call you even though your on the same ship with her and can't do it yourself??? Did I understand that correctly?? Very strange. I won't do that...

Colin begins with the *ad hominem* attacks against Mike:

On May 17, 2010, at 11:52 PM, MiGGY MIGGY miggymiggy wrote:

if you were in my shoes-- you'd want to make this trip a success
15000 USD is I believe more than half of your annual salary as a performer
I am able to do this bcos I am a military aviation consultant but it is still money
Leandra has to respect this why has she not logged into facebook for more than 2.5 weeks?
I have emailed her parents to no reply.
her parents are not quite so pc literate-- at least her mother is not.
you tell me what to do.

Mike takes the bait:

Date: Mon, 17 May 2010 21:24:12 -0700
From: mhogan80
Subject: Re: hi MIKE HOGAN-- Leandra Ramm
To: spitzers50

Dude. You don't know what I make! I make way more than some $30,000 a year! I own my own real estate investment company as well as a full time actor. Trust me I make way more money than u! Talk abt what u know!!

Colin parries and thrusts:

On May 18, 2010, at 1:51 AM, MiGGY MIGGY miggymiggy wrote:

Michael

it is 150K plus bonuses.
what I know is that Leandra was so broke at one stage-- owing the bank 400 USD and she asked me to cover it.
not only did I always cover her-- but I have always sent her amounts more than she asked. Why don't you ask her this?
you tell me if I deserve what I am experiencing now.

Mike-- either you make that call to her parents and ask what is happening or email Leandra
I am a military aviation consultant. I move amongst generals, pilots, intelligence and special operations personnel who give me no bullshit or nonsense. There is no reason why I must accept any from Leandra whom I hold and expect a much higher standard.

I have reason to believe Leandra has not checked email for 18 days yet-- as she updates her facebook and twitter whenever she logs on. but she

130

probably saw my email the last time she logged in on 30th April. Its again I think bcos of massive workload.

I do not want to 'mete out punishment" on Leandra as I have travelled so long and far. I know Leandra was angry over a disagreement that we had-- and I have not seen her so angry before I boarded. Probably because of massive workload on board.

Love covers a multitude of sins as the bible says and does not remember past wrongs. I do not want to cancel a meeting with a record company I have set up for her. I do not want to call upon my contacts to cancel her up and coming radio show. I do not want to ruin Leandra at all but bless her. I do not want to call up her agent and threaten anything. I do not want to barge into the Green room and throw things against the wall, make a scene in the green room in front of her friends. I do not want to, though I have the right to cut funding to all current and future projects planned for her.

These are things for the common selfish, self-centered American man-- but I am not even American or WASP. I want to show her and her family I am different. Indeed I have signed letters to her parents stating that I would not attempt even to sleep with Leandra on board the ship with her.

All I am asking now is a reconciliation with Leandra. I am in fact demanding it given the fact that I have sacrificed so much time and money on this one relationship.

You love Leandra in a different sense from I do.

If you do love her even as a friend-- you would send her an email or make a call to her parents, again you have the number-- tell them I am on board now and she is within visual range of me and tell them to tell her to ask her to invite me to dinner which I will pay for. I do have her room number but I don't even want to go to her. She has to fulfill her promise of coming to me.

I am truly concerned Michael that you are not taking things seriously. Ask yourself what you want to happen and if you'd like to be a peacemaker. to doubt the sacrifice would be to doubt a victory here. As a soldier once and young, I value honor, integrity and honesty.

I do not want to teach either friend or foe the virtues I learnt in national service.

You now understand why it is fundamentally important for her to come to me and not the other way round and this is where you need to come in to 'encourage' her to do what is right. I am not a sugar daddy or just a plain charity giver to some unknown musician who keeps asking and never gives back.

You know what to do-- either you make that important call to her parents at once or send her a private message on facebook.

Date: Tue, 18 May 2010 05:11:32 -0700
From: mhogan80
Subject: Re: important
To: spitzers50

First of all...why are u telling me what u make?? Is that supposed to impress me?? I have made $150k on one real estate transaction before! What do mean by "mete put punishment" ???? U sound like a stalker. From what Leandra told me she has a boyfriend already and it's not u!! U sound like a stalker!! I emailed Leandra to warn her abt u. I told her u keep emailing me and to be careful. Pls stop emailing me u freak!!!

On May 18, 2010, at 9:06 AM, MiGGY MIGGY miggymiggy wrote:

tell her about MichaelWadeLee.com
tell her I do not want to talk to him unnecessarily
Leandra Erin Ramm owes me this specific meeting on the ship I am owed courtesy it was my deal with Leandra that if I was not treated with courtesy MWL would be punished-- Leandra was online 3 hours ago
she really owes me ell her NOT to f**k around with me and I can make a call or email to NYC to have him done.

Date: Tue, 18 May 2010 06:19:19 -0700
From: mhogan80
Subject: Re: important
To: spitzers50
Are u threatening to kill somebody!?!?!

On May 19, 2010, at 2:33 AM, MiGGY MIGGY miggymiggy wrote:

how is <Minor Daughter's Name Redacted>?
I do not need to elaborate Michael Hogan
you are a small time real estate person. not a multi millionaire-- act your part you 29 year old.

Date: Wed, 19 May 2010 05:33:47 -0700
From: mhogan80
Subject: Re: <Minor Daughter's Name Redacted>
To: spitzers50

Are u threatening my daughter?!?!?! Dude I will end u if u even think abt coming near my family!!! Stop going on my fb page to get info on me u moron! I'm not going to do what u want me to do so go to hell!

Colin backpedals but continues to insult and threaten. It's all part of the dance.

On May 19, 2010, at 8:54 AM, MiGGY MIGGY miggymiggy wrote:

HI Mike

no I did not go to your FB page as I don't even know how to add it.
forget the Leandra Ramm problem. I will handle it like a man. no violence on the subsidiary targets no arms, no beatings.

I will visit her after her performance tomorrow.

If you had made the call to her parents -- none of this would have happened. I would not have gotten angry.
Michael-- I respect and love Leandra very much as a person. We are just a couple that need to work things out after so long...

I would have preferred if you had not exaggerated your wealth. Don't act up-- we are all guys here. I was hoping you'd solve my problem. Leandra can be stubborn, yes... that happens in some girls. but she is the only girl I will ever love.

I know you earn probably at most 50K a year- you fathered a kid at 23 plus and then another one a short time later-- which means you probably did not have much wealth to invest in much. I don't have info on ur real estate ventures yet-- but its probably foreclosure flipping-- which is done often by retail investors and hard to make money.

I checked on your house value-- its not that big with a mortgage to cover. Also being African-American-- I have studied and worked in the US long enough to know most blacks aren't that rich. This is not a criticism. Rather an observation. The fact that you are an actor rather than a producer or investor in a film or play means that you don't know where the money is made yet.

I will marry Leandra Ramm by the end of the year-- and then we will send you an invitation to the wedding. thats the only way I will ever fund the rest of her career.

Michael Lets be friends-- I am tired of all this sh*t of fighting. Spiritually it is no good for us.

If I wanted you ended up dead I would have gotten my government servant friends in DoD and Pentagon to do so. I work for them on consultancy projects. Ask Leandra. we have a history together and I promise you -- she and I will work thru all this thick and thin with God's help. We are a strong minded couple with just a few problems. thats all there is.

On Thursday or Friday I will go to Leandra's green room with a bunch of flowers and get her to dinner.

this has been a great learning experience for all of us.

God bless you michael.

Date: Wed, 19 May 2010 06:55:31 -0700
From: mhogan80
Subject: Re: <Minor Daughter's Name Redacted>
To: spitzers50

Most of my money and real estate is owned by my corporation idiot! I own 8 companies. Clearly ur not a savvy investor or u would have thought of that! I never said I was rich! I said I made more money than u and I do!! My company grossed $1.2m the past two years. I don't make $50k a year u psycopath! I was just in LA buying a small business for $40k! Ur an ignorant asshole! Also I don't live in doylestown! Idiot! I don't flaunt my money. U say Leandra is ur gf but she has never met u! If ur so tough email me ur number and address so I can call u! If u go near Leandra u will be arrested! She is very aware of ur threats and so are the authorities!

Colin is in his element, provoking argument (thereby getting information) by deliberate misstatements, providing intimate details about Hogan's family, then turning the tables, and ultimately using his opponent's own words against him. In this case, using the most basic reverse psychology technique, he demands Hogan stop writing him. Mak could do this in his sleep.

From: MiGGY MiGGY miggymiggy
Subject: Please do not write to me anymore-
To: mhogan80
Date: Thursday, May 20, 2010, 4:27 AM

I am not going to fight Leandra any longer and my checks on your property have revealed that you have a low nett worth really. if you were serious show me your tax statement. hah you cannot produce it. your dressing also proves you are not a rich person.

btw how is your other daughter? is she fine? you don't have to talk about your company etc-- my interactions with blacks from the US and Africa have revealed that most of them have a lot of money-- in the air that is-- and they are like Nigerians who promise to wire you money over the internet. if you catch my drift.

I only want to settle my disagreements with Leandra in a loving way.

134

no doubt you have already talked to Leandra. She is not thinking right at the moment and not saying eveything to you and that heightens tensions.
what annoys me is that she does not like to state that yes she sinned against me. I am not going to hold this or any past against her.

Please do not write to me anymore-- my ex-biz partner was just like you-- always trying to befriend whites and other higher order ethnic groups in order to have herself perceived as upperclass. She even dated and f**ked a lot of Swedish men because of her low self-esteem. again I saw thru her eventually.
everything will come to light in due time. Same with Leandra and me.
nonetheless I think we both should stop talking.

I think you are basically a nice person, a sometime actor when you can afford the time and opportunity but I am dismayed by your lack of integrity with regards to your wealth.

I am going to ask Leandra also to stop being friends with you. It is not good for her as well.

In the meantime, Hogan growing quickly savvy, had socially engineered Mak. His aim was to collect as many viable threats as he could in order to convince the police that Mak was a viable threat. Of one thing he was certain-- Mak needed to be put away.

On Thu, 5/20/10, MiGGY MIGGY miggymiggy wrote:
From: MiGGY MIGGY miggymiggy
Subject:
To: "Mike Hogan" mhogan80
Date: Thursday, May 20, 2010, 8:42 AM

by the way your wife's name is Jamila
no need to send back anymore emails to me or leandra
she has said she doesn't want to talk to you at all now
if I hear of you or from you again
I will send a representative who will wait for you and Jamila at your door with a nightstick.

Mike was black, which delighted Colin, who considered any race other than his own fair game. As he commonly did to bolster his outrageous statements, he fabricated my involvement and tacit acquiescence with his hateful nonsense.

From: spitzers50
To: spitzers50
Subject: mch-- STOP EMAILING ME OR LEANDRA IF U ARE WISE
Date: Thu, 20 May 2010 08:36:23 +0000

<Minor Daughter's Name Redacted>
...is your other daughter
look bro stop emailing me and Leandra anymore.
you are no longer her friend next time I hear from you
I will get my representative -- also a nigger to deliver groceries to your wife.

I am like Ariel Sharon-- he said 'my enemies know me well and I know them
even better. I need not elaborate'
you ni**ers don't learn that fast enough.
so please stop emailing me and Leandra ramm anymore.

I am sorry for sounding racist-- but Leandra says she does not like ni**ers
too! ;)

Mike forwarded me all these emails. Although he joked
about Colin's racism, I suspected it hurt him, probably even
created doubt about me. That was Colin's goal—
simultaneously to misdirect conversations while instilling
uncertainty, to discredit the truth and change it.

Michael Hogan mghoan80
Fw: STOP EMAILING ME OR LEANDRA IF U ARE WISE
May 20, 2010 9:54 AM

See below he threatened my other daughter. I didn't know you hated ni**ers
Leandra!!!! LOL!!
Michael Hogan

Parallel Victim Pools

Colin easily skipped between Singapore and Hong Kong. He'd been living in Hong Kong much of 2007 and 2008, emailing me often. To prove his whereabouts, he attached seemingly random photos ranging from "designer bathrooms," at Hong Kong's Lane Crawford shopping mall to dried chicken meat at a Hong Kong stall, to him and his "friends" hanging out.[109] Proving pieces of a story, like his being in Hong Kong, would persuade me that the accompanying fabrications were true, too, interspersing granules of truth among the many lies he propagated. I'm sure he sent me the photos to flaunt how freely he traveled internationally, despite his criminal conviction and the supposed confiscation of his passport. Another intimidation tactic demonstrating that the plebian rules didn't apply to him.

I think in his arrogance, though, his photos revealed more than he had contemplated—other victims or potential victims of his grifts. By looking at the dates and times on the emails and attached photos, I learned that while in the midst of attacking an ever-expanding group of people in my life, Mak was simultaneously stalking victims unrelated to our dynamic and previously unknown to me.

Posing as a professional photographer, Colin's penchant was for pouty-faced teenaged models, a vulnerable group, susceptible to flattery. He sent me their photos, sad-eyed, dressed in lingerie, desperate for recognition. I suspect the girls, who were unknown and had no money, were potential love interests, not financial marks. To make money, he'd continue with the photographer ruse from a different perspective, insinuating himself into the lives of unsuspecting retail business owners of hair salons, fashion boutiques, and jewelers, then extorting them.

Hong Kong Harassment

It turns out that in 2009, Hong Kong, Mak pled guilty to a count of criminal intimidation of a female jewelry merchant, who had turned down his business proposal. Mak and the victim had become acquainted in a Lan Kwai Fong bar. Posing as a photographer, he sent the victim an email offering to take photos of her jewels in exchange for HK$60,000. Once the victim declined, Colin escalated, threatening "to unleash dog/s to f**k her or she would get her raped."[110] He sent her another email, threatening her with a nightstick, an ominous promise he would later repeat in my case, against me, Michael Wade Lee, and others. Hong Kong took immediate action after the victim filed her complaint, arresting Colin by tracing his IP address.

Once I learned about Colin's arrest, I wrote Hong Kong police in offering my support.

To whom it may concern,

My name is Leandra Ramm. I am a US citizen. I am an actress and singer and have had a fair share of publicity on international Television. Over the past 4 years, a Singapore/Hong Kong citizen I believe, has been stalking me. His name is "Colin Mak Yew Loong" and he has a criminal record. I saw an online article that he was arrested for threatening another woman in Hong Kong and was arrested in October. I have thousands of emails to prove his threatening ways and illegal activity. I can forward you some of those emails or anything you need. Is there anything you can do to help me? Please see the articles below that show his past crimes. Thank you in advance for your help and I look forward to your reply.[111]

Hong Kong contacted me on May 11, 2010 with what would soon become a familiar refrain—no jurisdiction over Mak:

Dear Mr. (sic) Ramm,

The Judiciary of the Hong Kong Special Administrative Region only handles cases filed in courts of Hong Kong through the proper judicial channel. The matter you mentioned in your e-mail does not come within our jurisdiction. We are therefore not in a position to assist.

However, please consider approaching the Hong Kong Police Force by referring to the following website for the necessary information:[112]

Blog Warning

Colin Fritz Tan was infamous in at least one Hong Kong blog—elle.com.hk. In November 2008, Colin Fritz Tan was the topic of discussion—

Bitten:
2008 年 4 月 11 日 4:13 pm

Hi lisa and other ladies who may read this.Just to make you aware of a photographer called Fritz tang, who seems to have contacted you. Can you please not have any contact with him and definitely no photographs through him. He is an extremely nasty person who will try and post your pics on porn sites and link those sites to yours.I have had a very very nasty experience and would like to forewarn others.I shall send you a private email with more info.In the meantime please spread the word to all your friends to never interact with a guy called Fritz tang/Colin/

Hair Master   Hair Master :
2008 年 7 月 5 日 2:37 am

"Su Ling" then describes Fritz further.

fritz tang is one of the most mentally ill human beings that I have ever had to deal with, LADIES, MODELS AND ALL FELLOW HK PEOPLE BE AWARE, BE VERY VERY AWARE OF THIS MAN!!! I had the most shocking experience doing business with him and he is writing all these replies acting as different girls! Interpol is looking for him at the moment, he is running from singapore where he tried all the same tricks there and got burned at his own game. He is the one with the problem with porn and sex and gets furious when he cant get his way and as a result take that out on the people by telling lies and very sick ones on top of that. Do not believe a word he saying and phone the police when he wants to do any business.[113]

Unfortunately for me, I was already in the throes of Colin's attacks. The information did little except to confirm what I had long suspected. Mak was a recidivist predator who had been at this game for a long time.

Skye Boutique, Singapore

When I first contacted them in 2007, the Singapore Police Force cavalierly informed me that they had once arrested Colin in an unrelated stalking case. Inexplicably, given Singapore's "tough on crime" stance, Colin not only was still at it in 2010, but had greatly escalated his stalking. Turns out I wasn't his only victim.

Colin boasted of still another stalking incident, which never made it into the official police record. On February 24, 2010, the subject line of a forwarded chain of emails bragged, "I won in a settlement! By reason or force." The glee in his writing was evident. For once, Colin felt vindicated, although monetarily, his victory was laughably small.

The "dispute" concerned Skye Boutique, a small retail store, with high fashion aspirations. Colin set his sights on Skye's owner and proprietor, Ana Liew, whom he dogged until getting her to "settle" fabricated wrongs done him. She would be more fortunate than Nataliya Z., the Ukrainian model involved, who, like me, suffered Singapore police apathy and resistance.

Colin claimed that by using another photographer in a photo session with the model, both Ana and Nataliya violated certain business arrangements to which he claimed to be a party. He further asserted that Nataliya had worked with Skye Boutique behind his back, writing:

To think she collaborated with you to screw me.

I want you to know—that I was learning Ukrainian just in a short time specifically to get Nataliya's trust. I gained it. She was looking for assignments to tide over her financial crisis—I solved it for her through you by looking for assignments for her. I brought her to you for a casting and fitting.

After your assignment with Nataliya—she was due to model for another designer—but you have ruined that relationship more than enough already. She will never make it big as a model in Singapore anymore.

...My relationship with Nataliya is now ruined permanently—she went to the police for help though I offered her the same package deal as I have offered you—an apology or an exercise of strike options—however because my threats to her and her live-in boyfriend Sebastian R...were in Ukrainian and Russian which the police did not understand—they told her to f**k off and find a civil lawyer to sue me instead. It would have been the same if the threats were in English.[114]

Ana approached Colin's threats by apologizing to him and offering him a cash settlement. She wrote:

"I sincerely apologise for ruining your relationship with nataliya and for not informing you when I use her for my shoot. I used another photographer because he is a friend and his friend has a studio available at no cost. I did tell you I prefer a studio for the short. My decision is purely financial, it does not reflect your ability as a photographer."[115]

She then offered him $100 Singapore, equivalent to about $79 U.S. Liew was astute enough to recognize that Colin's gripe could be cheaply purchased, as long as she accorded him "face."

"I am willing to pay you as a peace offering and hope you will not be angry anymore. I have attached the agreement for your signature and will be left at the shop with the cheque by Friday. Hope you will be a gentleman and adhere to the terms of the agreement.[116]

Colin wrote back:

Dear Ana Liew—
Thanks for the email below and offer of settlement. I am glad you have come to a point where you choose to settle with me and come clean instead of "hiding.' It makes me feel much much better and all involved feel better. Its better to be at peace with you. Obviously.

It seemed an amazing value, and, I wondered, briefly, whether I could have made my nightmare go away for a flowery apology and a trivial monetary settlement. Probably not, given that Ana played a different role from Nataliya, who, like me, played the role of love interest in Colin's fevered imagination. The only thing that could replace me was another female romantic lead. Otherwise, given his recidivism, the only way to stop him was to capture and imprison him, with no possible access to the Internet.

True to form, in May 2010, Colin confirmed what I had suspected. Using a combination of English and Cyrillic, he wrote :

Dear Nataliya.
...I have left Singapore to be with my girlfriend in New York...I felt I had to talk to...you...to sort matters out now that I was in fact financially compensated by Anna Liew in January 2010 after much hassle in which she sent me a letter apologizing to me for her missteps. This happened after I repeatedly 'talked' to her 'nicely' about what legal actions I would take as I did the production, casting and negotiations. I accept that apology from her and accepted the compensation checque for the money. This is what I like to see. Humility."[117]

I was obviously the "girlfriend in New York," a typical Colin-fabrication. He would use similar ploys —trying to instill jealousy in me over a feigned engagement with a Brazilian model—with me once I had unequivocally stopped all communications with him. I prayed he would carry out his threats to "leave me" and envied Nataliya's reprieve.

What also struck me about this particular rant was his glee at humiliating others. Colin was, as his most loyal former friend Mona Hanson suggested, sadistic. He liked to watch his victims beg and apologize. That made him feel superior and that he had won whatever contest or dispute existed in his twisted mind. It probably also was a vestige from his abusive childhood, where he was made to stand out in the cold at age 3, was beaten and humiliated by his birth parents.

The Skye Boutique incident did offer a glimpse into Colin's logic. The fact was that he had won, albeit in a dispute of his own making, receiving both an apology *and* monetary compensation, albeit negligible. He would take those facts and aggrandize them, boast about his victory, and then fabricate other details.   In this way, Colin could lend credence to an otherwise fake life.

PART SIX
MINIONS

Disciples

Colin had gathered an online coterie of flesh-and-blood "friends": old college buddies, successful musicians, financial officers, lawyers, and international businessmen. For lack of a better term, I called them "minions," who would do him favors like calling me on the phone, inviting me to sing for a part, delivering gifts on his behalf.

As opposed to the multitude of Colin's self-proliferated fake identities, the minions were real people, possibly co-stalkers, maybe dupes. Perhaps varying degrees of both. Either way, these "minions" were a testament to Colin's social engineering skills. Either way, they bridged the gap between the virtual and physical world. Colin could get to me through real people.

The Inscrutable One: Gregory Singer

Not only was he internationally famous, he had some impressive connections in the world of classical music and in Hollywood. Yet Greg Singer, the first of Colin's minions, was perhaps the most damaging to me. In convincing me of Colin's harmlessness, urging me not to fear Colin, he provided a false sense of security. The sense I got from Singer was that Colin could be reasoned with.

I still wonder how Mak motivated Gregory into offering Singer Fine Violins as the venue for my creepy audition, and whether he even listened to my aria or was solely interested in my appearance. Either way, I'm convinced that Gregory's nod of approval was the impetus for my stalker to continue pursuing me.

Even if Singer was simply appeasing Colin by holding the "audition," why would he bother? How did my stalker get important people to do his bidding?

Subway Encounter

As fate would have it, I saw Singer one more time, in a random subway encounter late summer, 2007. I noticed him on the subway platform before he got on the 1 train at 86th Street.

We were both on our way downtown—I on the way home from rehearsal at the Martina Arroyo Foundation: *Prelude to Performance*. I played Dorabella, one of the leads.

Greg and I exchanged "hellos," then I reminded him who I was. He remembered me, asking, "Do you still keep touch with that Colin fellow?"

I said something like, "Oh my God, he is ruining my life! He's stalking me like crazy!"

He replied, "Don't worry about him, he is harmless. Just ignore him." I told him that I couldn't just ignore it, that it was horrible. Again, Singer reassured me, "Honestly, he is nothing to worry about." A little too conveniently, he disembarked at the next stop.

I guess I'll never know what Singer knew about Colin, and why he said the things he said to me and why he acted on Colin's behalf, especially given his claims that he barely knew Colin, having met him only a few times.

Despite making light of Colin's dangerous proclivities, it turned out that immediately after his train departure, Singer reported our encounter to Colin, which Colin then reported to me, angrily demanding I apologize. As usual, I wasn't sure what I'd done wrong but by then I was beyond trying to make sense of his warped thought processes.

Colin's call had the intended effect, which was to reveal his continuing influence over Singer. I couldn't argue with facts—how else would Colin know about the train, and so quickly at that. There was no other explanation.

Again I felt the gnawing doubt I'd had about Singer at the time of the audition—that the two of them were stalking together, having some sort of perverse leader and wingman relationship. That scared me.

I'm certain Colin relished my fear and basked in the power it bestowed on him.

The Co-Conspirator: Tony Thille

The real Tony Thille was an associate of Colin's in a Swedish company, Protec Consulting Co. & RusAvia Group, an exporter of "new and second hand Russian Mil and Kamov helicopters and also second hand Russian Fighter Aircrafts,"[118] with a Singapore Web address. Given Protec Consulting's trade, it wasn't too surprising that Thille and Colin were involved in weapons dealing, the subject of a recent criminal trial in Singapore. Tony, or more likely Colin purporting to be Tony, asked him to stop all contact. He wrote to us, warning that Colin might be in the U.S. and that I was in danger.

I had my doubts about the authenticity of Tony Thille, beginning with his lousy English, a language mastered by most Swedes. On the other hand, his stilted syntax was uniquely different from Colin's, and probably not easily imitable, even for a linguist like Mak, who dabbled in different tongues.

The point was that my stalker and the real Tony Thille dealt Russian weapons to Syria through Bulgarian thugs, which pushed Colin's terrorism from mere fantasy about killing to the credible threat zone. Surely, the FBI would react to death threats from an illegal arms dealer with terrorist ties!

Or, not so much.

The Most Loyal: Mona Hanson

Gregory Singer was passive-aggressive—he didn't want to engage. Colin seemed to have thrust Singer into the role of mute recipient, copied on Mak's emails to me, but never responding. Similarly aloof at the audition, his role was bemused, possibly amused observer who claimed not to know Colin very well. I learned after our subway encounter, of Singer's additional role, that of stealth informant. Either way, Singer's dynamic was only with Colin, not with me.

Mona Hanson was just the opposite: a brash attorney who knew Mak personally, probably better than anyone else in his life at the time. And she was willing to go to bat for him. From the tone of the emails she'd send me later, I surmised her interest in Colin was more than platonic.

The first time I heard from Mona was a phone call, where she unabashedly led me to believe that she was not only a friend, but represented Colin in a legal capacity, an image which didn't quite jibe with her decidedly non-legal Web site, an import-export company out of Hong Kong called *Trendy Living*.

Her call came at the end of January 2007, from a Virginia phone number, the same as that listed on her *Trendy Living* site. At the time, I was living in North Carolina, an "artist in residence" at Opera Carolina. Beginning with her premise—that Colin was innocent of illegal arms dealing—I found her over-the-top and dubious.

Identifying herself as "one of Colin's friends" she said, "You know, he's a really good guy you have there," that I should call Colin so he could explain his true role in the arms dealing case. She maintained that what I read in the papers was false. It was important that I know what a "good guy" he was, she reiterated. "Don't get the wrong idea about him." If anything, her phone call was evidence that Colin had duped another person into believing he and

I were somehow romantically connected, making him less, not more, credible in my eyes.

In well-timed "closer" fashion, Colin "coincidentally" emailed me shortly after Mona and I hung up. He began with, "Thanks for picking up the call from my attorney friend Mona Hanson," hoping I'd believe he retained a *consigliere*, that he was that important. As usual, his email contained half-truths, muddying the waters enough to make his version of the story believable. He said nothing more about Mona, but copied her on the email.

Mona would later write me that Colin had boasted about getting his visa to the United States renewed based on his heroic actions in getting the *real* arms dealer, named Chaandrran, convicted. "I had to meet in Thailand because (of) my promises to the Singapore secret service that I would not conduct sensitive assignments in Singapore anymore—even with United States Government personnel.

Colin went even further, offering me to meet his CIA case officer, to see me at the Pentagon and, ultimately responding to the MWL cease-and-desist letter, threatening Michael Lee with his expanded powers under the Patriot Act, calling himself a protected witness by the U.S. government. "My partner Tony Thille and I have the USAF/Pentagon as our clients for our consulting projects hence our duty to inform them of Syrian mischief." Colin said he was on an S-visa to testify against the Syrian representative in a U.S. Federal court." It was a surreal story, with some truth buried in it.

In the end, none of his prevaricating even if true, would change my overriding feeling that Mak was unstable and dangerous and that I never wanted to hear from him again. I knew I had to sever all ties with this guy once and for all.

--For Your Eyes Only

Almost one year after she had first contacted me, I heard from Mona again, both on the phone and in increasingly dramatic emails. In her phone call, she told me that Colin was stalking her and contacting her employers, that he wasn't a good guy at all, he had been ruining her life, and she planned to cut him out permanently.

The Subject line said simply, "Colin," and it had been sent at 3:57 a.m.

Hi Leandra,

Hi how are you? This is Mona, a colleague of Colin Mak, I don't know if you remember speaking to me on the phone? I really need to discuss something important with you. For a long time, I was trying to decide whether I should contact you or not however I think it may be in your best interest to speak to me. If you are interested in doing this, can you email me and let me know. I would appreciate if you would keep this between us.

Mona

I had spoken with Mona several months earlier, more than enough communication for me. What more was there to say, and why bother? Having at this point experienced a solid year of stalking and harassing emails from Colin, I had been programmed to doubt the veracity of any email. This email could very well be Colin; the syntax was strange. I just wasn't sure. Colin had even managed to impersonate me quite believably. So, as I had been advised by law enforcement, I ignored it.

Mona sent her next and final email of 2007 at 4:12 a.m. on December 8, 2007, about 48 hours later. The purpose was to unburden herself of guilt in colluding with Colin against me and to prove to me that she had cut ties with him. The subject line was, generically paranoid, "FOR YOUR EYES ONLY."

Hi Leandra,[119]

As you can tell by the time, I couldn't sleep because of the events of the last 72 hours, just received email from someone regarding Colin. This is for your information, although you refused to say anything much to me—, I sent you this because I truly hope that no one has to go through what I did with this guy. He keeps on involving you in various emails to different people so you may become involved in this but that will not be because of me.

I don't expect a reply from you.

I have not told him we spoke nor that I sent this email to you do I ever plan to – you have my word on that. I hope this is my last communication with him.

Keep safe,
Mona[120]

I wondered what Colin had done to inspire the email, whether Mona had been drinking, whether she was playing me again.

--Mona's Cease and Desist

Attached to Mona's "For Your Eyes Only" email was the email she had written to Colin on December 7, 2007 around 7 a.m., subject: "Cease and Desist." She sent the email to warbird5k, Colin's official email address, but she also sent it to Miggy Miggy. I found that odd, Mona acknowledging Miggy, whom I assumed was a clandestine persona, unique to Colin's correspondence to me.

A new possibility emerged. I wondered whether Mona could be Miggy. Her histrionics, prior collusion with Colin and fierce loyalty to him, plus her admission of guilt, all indicated that she participated in Colin's fraud on me— maybe even cloaked by one of his emails. Claiming she "was no victim," she wrote him:

Even with all of this on the guise of friendship etc., I take my part of the blame because I enabled you and put up with it even when I tried numerous times to cut you off – you resorted to your emotional blackmail which I fell for each time.[121]

After reading Mona's ensuing cease-and-desist letter to Colin, I concluded that Mona was instead Colin's victim, not a co-stalker. Colin had plummeted in her estimation from "good guy" to incorrigible stalker, destroying her life and triggering her to write a cease–and-desist letter of her own. Cruel irony, indeed!

The Cease and Desist letter began:

This is my final email to you. Ever since I have known you when you didn't get your way, you have become abusive, threatening and just plain vengeful and dangerous. You have called me the worst of names, become obsessive and shown definite times of complete dementia.

It was as if Mona were speaking from my own voice; her letter continued to both fascinate and horrify me at the same time. She described in detail the Colin I'd grown to know—a relentless predator, who at first acted generous, giving gifts, offering to be my sponsor, misrepresented to both of us the nature of his various "business" relationships and "friendships" to gain credibility.

Below, Mona, referring to Colin's arms dealing conviction as his "problem in Singapore," summarizes her reasons for ending the friendship. Colin's pushing gifts and money, followed by outraged demands for payment and apologies, was an all-too-familiar tactic. I believed her.

Even after all of this, we didn't talk for some time and when you reappeared you seemed to be a different person so I chose to start over with you. When I found out about your problem in Singapore, I was one of the only friends who stood by you, heard what you said and chose to believe you period. I suppose somehow it must have been partially due to the fact you had been so generous (seemingly to me), it truly touched my heart and I appreciated it. Funnily enough, you were the one who offered your help to me numerous times, which I turned down and finally accepted your gift . This gift was taken on a few presumptions that seemed to be facts from you. 1) No strings attached, 2) You had plenty of money as you kept saying, 3) You always helped your friends out (Leandra, Tosheffs) and that you wanted no thanks, no credit etc. it was something that made you happy. I numerously thanked you and tried to show you my appreciation through actions. That is why after hearing your side of the story and seeing the papers etc. and you begging for me to call Leandra, someone I didn't even know, and talk to her, I went ahead and did so.

I learned more. Colin had told Mona he was getting a renewed visa to the United States based on information he had gathered during the arms dealing excursion. The U.S. government had denied Colin's visa request back in 2005, according to this email exchange between Colin and a purported government official, John Doe:[122]

Dear Mr. MaK,

First and foremost, thank you for your desire to assist with our common goals. Unfortunately, at this time we are unable to facilitate your request for a US Visa, this is an issue that is not negotiable. I would like to thank you again for your efforts and would simply request that if you are ever in possession of any critical information in the future, that you contact one of our official representatives in your area.

Respectfully,

JD

Hanson confirmed his tricks and what I had long suspected, that Colin was not harmless. She had deluded herself into believing his crazy yet innocuous nerd act. Gregory Singer also called Colin harmless, and I had believed him. Colin had fooled all of us, masking "the real Colin," whom Mona highlights below:

But then the real Colin showed up again, back came the clear signs of instability: threatening emails, sexually deviant communication and emails, etc., when you didn't get what you perceived you wanted. I put up with this behavior for a few reasons, I felt at that point you were harmless, full of hot air and in some sick way I felt a loyalty towards you because you had helped me out. At that point, I didn't feel like you were dangerous, I was clearly wrong. You proceeded to make threats on people's lives, claiming to either physically inflict bodily harm (Leandra's fiancée, the German guy) or destroy someone's life (Leandra's, mine, etc.) I was actually surprised because the lengths you were willing to go because someone said a few things that hurt you really scared me. You actually wanted to commit a crime because of a few words or teach someone a lesson who you had also helped out with money because they didn't respect you? I actually had to calm you down and speak reason with you about Leandra. You actually plotted to do certain things to certain people . Who plots these things? It is not normal. You also plotted to hack certain banks and tried to employ me to find a hacker for you —of course that was met with complete silence or amusement on my part. I could go on and on – but again what's the point?

I wondered how many more victims existed beside Mona and me.

You even have become obsessed with random girls on the Internet, girls you would tell me about that I knew you would fantasize about... It was very disturbing...

Mona's At-Bay Attempt

Earlier in 2007, Colin (as Miggy Miggy) had written me from Hong Kong, bragging about his nights out with a Russian musician and Russian pilots who liked to get drunk. He had his new Russian friend send pictures. Although he was portraying a life full of excitement jet-setting (almost literally, given his obsession with pilots and aeronautics) Colin was actually living at Mona's Hong Kong apartment, sleeping on the floor. She wrote,

You have nooo idea how hard it was for me to see all of this because I did care for you as a friend very much so, that is why I basically took care of you in Hong Kong, let you sleep on my floor (after you literally forced yourself into my room with your suitcase, etc.), bought your meals and gave you money. I couldn't let you be on the streets. Again, I felt some sort of loyalty even after everything you did to me. Yes a couple of times you were sweet to me but I soon realized that was with an agenda. If someone does what you want them to do then great, if someone says something contrary to what you want to hear, you simply don't hear it or you hear it and exact revenge.

Like me, Mona had already tried to pull away from Colin, unsuccessfully, saying "I was pulling away from you and tried to cut things off completely and then you would hold the money that you gave as a gift to me over my head and I chose to feel guilty about it."

Mona then attempted her own version of what I'd later describe as an "at bay" solution, meaning keeping him away from her with some controlled interaction, in this case by employing him at her company. That didn't work either. Colin took the job readily enough, but as is the wont of a cyberstalker, did nothing to keep his job, ultimately losing it.

I told you let's just continue business together (I felt the last vestiges of loyalty to you) and tried to coach you with certain things but you again showed no true business acumen nor was willing to learn anything and only would come up with truly bizarre suggestions for business etc. When Thomas got involved, he saw all of these traits in you and the way you interacted with us, I tried to help you numerous times because I did believe that if you

158

continued the way you were going, that you would be removed... You were removed from the project Colin because you simply put no effort into it AT all except with your random emails that had nothing to do with anything we were doing and your broken promises and you not keeping Thomas abreast with what was going on. You accepted that a few months ago and so this reaction to it now is simply bizarre.

The aftermath of losing his position would be extreme, but not unexpected.

Breaking the Golden Rule

Mona's 2007 cease and desist letter showed Colin's template of tactics and behaviors. She tried to appeal to Colin's better nature, finally realizing that he was incapable of certain emotions, primarily empathy. Colin would never "do unto others," nor would he anticipate or care about karmic retribution. I think that's what finally convinced Mona to cut Colin from her life.

In 2007 she wrote:

There are way too numerous list of things I could talk about but it serves no purpose? Why? Because you are one of the people that absolutely does NO self reflection, it is everyone else's fault things are the way they are and any perceived lack of respect etc. is met with vengeance, threats of reprisal, hysteria, etc. I have numerous, numerous communications with you to prove this and frankly was warned along time ago from people who knew you that you were unstable but they never knew to what extent. I guess I was one of the lucky ones to constantly see this side. In fact what s really sick a few times is you would get "turned on" by all of this craziness. And as I told you many times before, I refuse to be a part of that. You have simply not learned the GOLDEN rule in life: For every action, there is an effect, good, bad or ugly.

Death Threats for Mona

By the time of her last contact with me, in April 2008, I was pretty certain that Mona was unbalanced, obviously attracted to Colin which avowed an unnatural "loyalty" to him, causing her to go great lengths to "save" him from himself. Although hyperbolic, I was certain that she, like I had experienced the ranting anger in Colin's threats and stalking.

Her final email to me was another strange one, and as in the email from December 2007, the subject line was "URGENT—FOR YOUR EYES ONLY."

The beginning, too, was similar, reading, "I don't know whether you remember me, we talked a while back regarding Colin." I found that weird—obviously, I remembered her. I wasn't likely to forget Mona, her vehement defense of Colin, and her subsequent flip-flopping. Now she wrote:

"... I did try to warn you about him but you were extremely aloof to me regarding him. My family and I as well as my previous business partner have now been receiving death threats from him and I have reported him to the authorities officially-.

By "previous business partner," she likely meant "Thomas," who had fired Colin from the import business in Hong Kong—a job Mona had secured for Colin.

I believed that Mona was telling the truth about the stalking. I just wasn't sure whether the rest was true. Cryptic references to "government agencies" and police reports with no number or even country reference made her seem paranoid.

If you need the police report number let me know, the officials have now dragged in higher authorities because of the nature of these crimes. I can't say much more to you for a few reasons, one being that this is EXTREMELY serious (government-wise) and I can't trust that you won't say anything to him. However, I am going out on the line right now to let you know because if he has done this to me, he may do the same to you and I know you had a situation with him where he was irate before. He has made up so many lies regarding me and the treatment of him especially regarding the money he sent me. He says that you are now his fiancé and you are getting married at the end of the year. Because of this you will be contacted by the police and some other authorities. Since I know that he is delusional and found out that he has even worse of a history than I found out before, I don't believe that you are together which only indicates to me that he is now obsessing over you and it could become dangerous. If it is true, then you really need to watch yourself. I forwarded most of the emails I get from him to the agents and police.

On the other hand, given Colin's capacity for social engineering and disruption of the status quo, Mona could have been legitimately scared enough to contact "government authorities" and circumspect about publishing information that I could forward to Colin. Although I knew the ridiculousness of Colin's claims about our supposed engagement, Mona didn't—perhaps she thought he and I were aligned as a team, something I had believed about her and Colin. Certainly, Colin played to her insecurities, muddying the truth to get his way.

Previously uncertain, ultimately, I concluded that Mona, not Colin, wrote the emails sent to me from her "trendyliving.com" domain, although arguably as Mona's roommate, Mak could have had access to her computer and account passwords. The syntax, however, convinced me that he was not the email's author. Colin's English was not accomplished enough to replicate an attorney's writing style and grasp of the language.

Regardless of its authenticity, I refused to respond. I just didn't trust anyone. Why should I trust her? What could I do for her? I felt bad for her but by that time was in survival mode; I had to protect myself.

As part of her final email to *me,* Mona forwarded me Colin's last email to *her*, replete with accusations of nonpayment and extortion threats—the usual Mak fare. And, of course, there were the delusional references to our (mine and Mak's) pending nuptials. By now I was pretty certain that Mak believed the more he repeated a published lie, the closer it resembled truth. Mak had written,

You may contact me at this email address. and I make it wonderfully clear to you that I DO EXPECT TO BE PAID. I need it to get married to my fiancee Leandra and it is my late Aunt's money given to me. Should you ignore this request of repayment... I don't have to fear. God will annihilate your family with barrenness, death, disease and destruction. I know you are also a Christian-- this has happened many times to the enemies of Israel. I have asked God to unleash the forces of hell on your family because you have returned good for evil.   Don't get f**ked Mona.

Mona closed the final email in a cautionary, slightly hysterical tone—very different from her first contact with me, where she effusively and recklessly defended Colin, trying to convince me about what a great guy he was:

I am not BSing, playing games, lying or whatever and have proof to back this up. I wanted to let you know and tell you that most likely you will get contacted because of this. If I hear no response from you or you let him know of this email then I will be able to tell once again that you haven't taken me or this seriously and you will put my family and I more in danger.
Mona

In the end, though, no one from "the government" ever contacted me about Mona, nor did I ever hear from her again.

Brian Asparro: The One Who Should Have Known Better

Brian Asparro, handsome, well educated (a Northwestern graduate of the Kellogg School of Management), was a successful executive, and had done a lot of business in the Far East. Previously at Moody's, now working at a smart green startup company in New York, he was the minion who crossed the line. Mona had been eccentric and troubled, Tony Thille and Singer, probably duped. But until Asparro, no minion had the audacity to come into my physical realm.

Colin first referred to Brian in a 2008 email to me from Hong Kong:

"Leandra darling
Wellington Gallery has asked me to photograph their gallery...
I am charging them some 2000 USD jus for a day's work which is easy to do!
When I finish my work in HK and when you are ready to see me...I am flying back to the US with my American business partner Brian Asparro.[123]

In 2010, Asparro showed that Colin could reach beyond international borders, straight into my parents' home. Colin had done this before, with hundreds of voicemails, phone calls, gifts, and letters through the postal service. But this time, Colin used a person to reach me, to make contact. As with all of Colin's relationships, whether Asparro was a willing participant in Colin's stalking or an unwitting pawn is unclear. At the very least, given his position, business savvy, and age (born in 1976), he should have known better than to act on behalf of a convicted arms dealer. That fact was public record.

Indisputable is that Brian Asparro hand-delivered a bouquet of pink flowers to the bellman at my parents' cooperative in New York on July 30, 2010, at approximately 9:05 p.m. Building security cameras captured his image and although my dad ran out after him, Asparro disappeared into the New York swarms.

Along with the flowers, I received a letter, written the day before my 26th birthday. It made me sick, especially his twisted protestations of love:

Silvestra...

If you received this-it means my friend from my Hong Kong days. He is a trusted American friend of mine.

I still love you with every bit of my heart. Lets forget about what happened in the past—it is implortant for us to move forward. I think about you often even though I am so far away. I care about you deeply.

I am going to the Seychelles soon to complete my missions with the Royal Marines...it is an important and dangerous contract with the UK government . I am the commanding officer...

I guess in times like these—it is so much more important for me to think about the ones I love and care about the most. I do not want to die without marrying you. I have never looked at or loved any other girl as much as I have for you.

Please email back soon to allay my fears.
Colin the warbird!
26th July—Singapore.[124]

I have tried to track Asparro, finding him on social networks, discovering his marital registry online—engaged to a woman from Hong Kong with a wedding date scheduled for December 2012. Although we have made many attempts to get his side of the story, he has failed to account for his actions that day in New York, or respond in any way. Why would he deliver flowers on behalf of Colin? Was he a dupe or a co-stalker? Was this a case of "no good deed goes unpunished"? Or was he in league with the devil?

All I know for sure is that Asparro's delivery of those flowers to my parents' house on Roosevelt Island was one of the low points of my life. Despite finally cutting off all communications with Colin, something the police had assured me would end the stalking, Mak, through Asparro, had violated me in the most personal way.

Soon after the flowers were delivered that evening, I got an email from Colin with pictures that Asparro took of the outside of my parents' building. It was Asparro's way of proving to Colin he had done his job.

PART SEVEN
LAW ENFORCEMENT ODYSSEY

Peregrination

In Homer's classic, *The Odyssey*, it takes the protagonist Odysseus ten years to return home to Ithaca from Troy—a journey of only about 565 nautical miles.

My ongoing journey through the law enforcement maze began in 2007, has covered thousands of miles from North America to Asia to Europe. Yet the legal landscape hasn't much changed.

"On or about (March 2007) I also communicated with the Singapore Consulate and Embassy, United Nations, and private professionals for assistance. None of this helped. I had nowhere to turn. My career was ruined, I was losing work and therefore was financially struggling, and I was emotionally abused. This situation was affecting my career, the people I worked with, and scared others around me to the point where he was ruining everything that mattered for me concerning my work. The perpetrator threatened me and my family and my employers and my colleagues because he wanted me to talk and communicate with him/have a relationship with him."[125]

Authorities Have No Authority (Or So They Say)

"There's nothing we can do." I'm not exaggerating when I estimate hearing this line or some variation five thousand times since Colin first came into my life. If I can point to the one, overriding attitude of law enforcement, whether on a local or national level, it is that they are powerless (perhaps "impotent" is a better word?) to help a victim of cyberharassment, cyberbullying, even cyberterrorism. After all, Colin made thousands of credible, violent threats, describing the means (nightsticks, knives, guns, bombs) and the motive (a general sense of being wronged by the woman he loved), aggravated by uncontrollable anger and evidence of mental instability. And let's not forget the most compelling evidence of all—Colin's international arms dealing conviction! What more did they need?

Yet, for six years, every government official I contacted in Singapore and the United States refused to take my case seriously, or to get involved at all.

There is a line from the Old Testament, "The Wicked Flee Where None Pursueth."[126] This ancient cautionary proverb is an apt description of the general inertia surrounding the pursuit of cyberterrorists like Colin Mak. The Colins of the world have free rein to terrorize their victims, especially girls and women, to any degree of which they are capable, pretty much with impunity. The legal repercussions are slight to nonexistent. It's inevitable that stalkers, already sociopaths, will take the minimal risk of continuing to stalk and harass. Those are good odds for predators. They'll take their chances.

I do not fault law enforcement personnel for being stymied. They lack support, training, and tools. I do hold them responsible for their "nuts or sluts" mindset, however, an unforgivable attitude pre-dating current sexual assault victim laws. In other words, police categorized victims of cyberstalkers as either mentally ill ("nuts"), or as asking for it, ("sluts.") I've no doubt that this

169

mentality, coupled with the fact that I was insignificant (i.e., not a financial institution or important business figure) played a large role in the way they treated me.

Speaking for myself and the growing number of stalking survivors, I demand a higher standard.

Asking for Help: Repository Connection

After a year of Colin's terrorism and no response from traditional avenues, I reached out to David Plotz, author of *The Genius Factory*.[127]

David's book followed certain progeny of the Repository for Germinal Choice, now adults. Although not portrayed in the book, I appeared with David on news and talk shows, including *The View*, *Good Morning America* and, of course, *Anderson Cooper*. Those appearances caught Colin's attention.

In light of this history, I thought it appropriate to contact David. As an author and journalist, he'd be interested in the story. And, as editor of Washington, D.C.-based Slate.com, Plotz surely had influential relationships with high-ranking government officials.

On January 26, 2007, I wrote David:

"This is very scary... this situation with Colin. Colin Mak is the man that saw me on CNN last year and was in contact with me via email. After I became suspicious of him, I asked him to please stop contacting me and he didn't."[128]

I explained how Colin contacted Chelsea Opera and other companies and described the call I had received from Mona Hanson, "his attorney," protesting Colin's innocence in the Singaporean arms dealing case. I finished with:

"I just don't know what to do at this point. What do you suggest? I am very scared and just don't want anything to do with this man....I just don't want to be involved with him at all. I very much appreciate your opinion on this matter."

David responded a couple of days later:

"I still think the best policy is avoidance. He may try to bother you with phone calls or phone calls to opera companies, but he will get tired of it if you ignore him...If you're worried, place an extra security code on your bank accounts, change your cell phone number, etc. But I do think ignoring will have the most beneficial long term effect. If this continues, I will try to put you in touch with Washington authorities who might have a thought. But, realistically, I think he's just a pest, and best ignored."[129]

When I wrote him back in spring 2007, even though I had taken Plotz's advise to ignore him, Colin's communications had, instead of dying off, increased in number and escalated in violence. In the meantime, I had contacted the Manhattan field office of the FBI, the Singapore Police Force, and the NYPD, to no avail.

--Friends in High Places

In spring 2007, as promised, David contacted his friends in law enforcement:

Hi Leandra

I heard back from the first of two of my high up law enforcement friends. This is from a friend who is extremely high in the ___. He consulted with several colleagues, including a top CIA official and the head of the NYPD's terrorism/intelligence unit.

First, they believe he is almost certainly a crazy, delusional person. He will eventually lose interest in you.[130]

Plotz then conveyed the "friend's" instructions on how to handle Colin:

- I should communicate to Colin that I had contacted an attorney and law enforcement officials, and that he should never contact me again in any way.

- I should then change my email accounts.

- From that point, I should never again respond to anything he sends. (Actually, I should never have responded in the first place—and should not do so if anything like this should come up again.)

- I should print and save all the emails that he sent, document all prior interaction, which I should email that to the Singapore National Police. David offered to find an address for evidence submission.

In closing, he said:

"If these steps don't have the desired effect, there are a few more, elaborate steps we can take. My friend is close to the Deputy Prime Minister of Singapore, who is also the country's minister of National Security. If the Singapore Police don't respond to your request, my friend might be able to mention it to the minister. In addition, there is a NYPD officer posted to the Singapore National Police. If necessary, my friend can notify him of your problems, and he would also be able to get the Singapore Police to act. These

are extreme steps, which he would only take if you have no success with the measures outlined above."
Best
D[131]

Unable to sleep, I wrote Plotz early the next morning:[132]

Dear David,

Thank you so much for your email. I really appreciate your help with this situation. We have already taken the steps that your friend suggested. We have told him to cease all contact, we told him that we have taken legal action, we have not responded to any of his emails and he only has intensified his modes of attack.

The actions of this individual have threatened and damaged my opera career and my boyfriend's career as well. This individual has unsettled and destabilized a major artist management company that represents us. This individual has created sever (sic) problems for most of the opera companies I have worked with. He has caused fear among various opera employees and has threatened their well-being as well as my own. This individual has threatened us and the companies that he will show up at specific opera performances and cause us physical harm, also putting the companies at risk. This individual has caused significant problems, fear and damage to the opera community. In addition, he is also emailing my parents every other day, now threatening harm to my family as well. We have documentation for all of this.

Colin Mak is a known stalker. We (the police and FBI) are all aware of his dangerous criminal record. He was arrested at Harvard University for stalking and was prosecuted and jailed for international arms trafficking of illegal weapons in foreign countries. We have every reason to be alarmed and afraid of what might happen in the future. By every account, he is an unbalanced and dangerous man. We have exhausted every national official means to stop this. The FBI has a file on this case, but unfortunately they can not help up further as this is out of their jurisdiction. We are now appealing to you as our only way to stop this impending crisis.

I would like to take the additional steps you mentioned. I would like to send the emails to the Singapore National Police and get it to the Legal Attache in the US Embassy in Singapore. We are at the point where we have to do something like this. If your friend can get us an address I would greatly appreciate it. I think it is necessary for us to mention this to the Prime Minister of Singapore as well and we should also contact the NYPD officer posted to the Singapore National Police.

I know these are extreme steps, but they have to be taken. This crazy man is trying to ruin our careers and lives and some companies and people, unfortunately, are listening to him. In addition, this has caused me so much emotional distress. I have to constantly do damage control and explain this situation to all of these companies. I can't ignore this anymore; this has to stop, and it has to stop asap. I hope you and your friends can help us take these next steps. Thank you again so much for your advice and attention to this matter, David. I really appreciate it. I look forward to hearing from you again soon. Fell free to forward this letter to the appropriate authorities.

Regards, Leandra

A few hours later, David responded:

Hi Leandra

I will ask my friend to get you a contact from Singapore national police and the legal attaché in the embassy. I am not going to ask him to check with the Minister or talk to the NYPD officer yet. Those are more extreme steps, and too large a favor to ask yet. I expect that Singapore Police and the legal attaché will respond promptly and effectively, and you won't need any more than that. If that proves entirely ineffective, I will check with my friend for the larger favor.[133]

Visiting the Bureau

Early in 2007, Michael Wade Lee and I visited the New York FBI field office at the Federal Plaza, armed with emails, call logs, and witness statements.

"I brought all the evidence I had and was assigned to Agent Alan Reichert (newyork@fbi.gov). After a couple of weeks' investigation, Agent Reichert told me to ignore the emails; they are out of the FBI's jurisdiction."[134]

MWL and I still tried, sending the FBI emails like the one below. We just couldn't understand why they were so impassive. Surely, they couldn't refute the mounting evidence of death threats, like the following:

From: Miggy M mailto:spicekits130
Sent: Saturday, May 19, 2007 7:03 AM
To: info
Subject: HI AMERICAN OPERA PROJECTS

YOU CAN TELL MICHAEL WADE LEE-- YOUR FORMER TENOR THAT WE WILL SHOOT HIM IN THE HEAD WITH A .45 IF WE DO NOT RECEIVE AN APOLOGY FROM HIM

Mike forwarded the above to the FBI on May 22, 2007, imploring Agent Moore, another FBI agent we were in communication with, to take Colin (and us) seriously:

"Mr. Moore,
This looks like a death threat to me. What else do we need to stop this guy?
Mike Lee."[135]

Moore never even bothered to write back. Soon we'd become painfully familiar with the Bureau's blind eye/snarky raised-eyebrow response. We weren't the first "complainers" they'd dealt with.

FBI Fob Off

I had followed instructions of Plotz's high-ranking government insiders to no avail. It was time to escalate to the "more elaborate steps" David had earlier suggested.

Hi, David,
I just got this email from him now. I'm sorry to bother you with this but I don't' know what else to do or who else can help me. The FBI isn't doing anything and I am very scared for my safety. He put a picture of my family below this email and I just am very scared he is going to try and harm us ....[136]

Soon afterward, he forwarded me part of an email from his "friend":

"The FBI liaison officer in my office suggests that she to go a web site operated by the bureau: www.ic3.gov. She should input all the info she can gather on this situation—old emails, etc. on this matter and they should coordinate a response by FBI NY, LEGATT Singapore , etc. Please let us know if she does not get a response from that and we will check on it further."[137]

On May 5, I filed an IC3 complaint , the "web site operated by the bureau," ID I0705051408575001. I quickly received the automated (it was a Saturday) boilerplate response, describing IC3's mission, "To serve as a vehicle to receive, develop, and refer criminal complaints regarding the rapidly expanding area of cyber crime."[138]

My heart sank as I continued to read. The next line, and the rest of the letter, was a complete evasion of responsibility by IC3 and the FBI.

"The IC3 aims to give the victims of cyber crime a convenient and easy-to-use reporting mechanism."[139] I thought, cynically, that a means of reporting a crime was fine, but to what end? The next paragraph answered my question. It was an utter abrogation of responsibility, in the face of an admitted crisis of complaints—"thousands each day." Were these guys serious?

"Complaint Status:

The IC3 receives thousands of complaints each month and does not have the resources to respond to inquiries regarding the status of the complaints... Ultimately, investigation and prosecution are at the discretion of the receiving agencies."[140]

Of all the illusory nonsense I had ever seen (and being an entertainer, I had seen a lot), this was about the worst—pandering and placating, promising zilch.

The IC3 system, in a nutshell, was a microcosm of the cyber-crimes-against-individuals problem. The government, relying on the old "we don't have resources" line, offered instead an arena where we hysterical bitches could complain. That's all we needed, after all, was to be heard, "women are from Venus," right? We don't want solutions, just a shoulder to cry on!

In the meantime, things were getting worse with my stalker. I next wrote Plotz on May 8th:

"I spoke with the FBI but they don't seem to be taking me seriously. I doubt they will do anything to help me. They keep saying "Unfortunately, there is nothing we can really do. It's up to the US Department of Affairs office, and if they say no, we can't really do anything. Unless there is a death threat at a specific time and place we can't really step in."[141]

The FBI was also hesitant in reaching out to the legal attaché, a measure David's government "friend" had recommended. I told David that I doubted the FBI actually would do anything for me, based on the vibe I got when talking to them.[142]

Sure enough, the one time I had called the FBI and asked to speak with Officer Reichert, the response was predictably arrogant and lazy. The operator asked, "What's your reason for calling?"

I said, "I am a victim of a terrible cyberstalker who is sending me death threats."

She responded, "Honey, this is the FBI. We deal with real murders and homicide and terrorism every day, not emails. Just ignore it. I can't put you through to Officer Reichert for that."

Not surprisingly, I had again wasted my time with the FBI.

Singapore Sling

I recently learned that Interpol was planning to build the International Cyber Crimes Center in Singapore. What an irony, considering their consistent four-year evasion of any responsibility in my case, until, that is, A.J. Fardella orchestrated their possible loss of face. There have been more than three investigators since Black Diamond Data took the helm in 2011 and before that, countless others who only contacted me as a formality, and then only to alert me that I had no case.

"On or about (May, 2007) I contacted the Singapore Police. I filed an electronic police report, I spoke to officers on the phone, and emailed them. They said they could not help me since the crimes did not take place in Singapore. The Singapore Police Force Report Number is Report No. A/20070510/2062."[143]

I didn't have much faith in Singapore arresting Colin. I wrote Plotz, "I went to the Singapore Police website and will fill out a crime report, but again, I don't know if they will even respond to my request being that I am not a Singapore citizen."[144]

I was wrong. I did hear from Singapore, albeit in an automated email with subject line, "Singapore Police confirmation—report":

Your report has been forwarded to Central Police Division. Your report number is A/20070510/2062.

A copy of your report has been emailed to your given email address, LeandraRamm. Within the next 48 hours, the Police will also inform you of the name and contact number of the investigation officer in charge of your report.

If you do not receive your report or email from the police, please contact SPF Service Improvement Unit (SIU) at
Tel: 1800-3580000 or
Email: SPF_Service_Improv_Unit@.sg

It was a start.

The Feds, Again

Although the FBI had essentially wiped their hands clean of my case, Plotz's communications on my behalf seemed to motivate them, at least temporarily. About a week later, I got a call from the FBI: Singapore had changed its mind.

I wrote Plotz of the good news on May 15, 2007:

Hi David,

I haven't heard back from you yet, but I just wanted to write you to let you know I did get a call back from the New York FBI office today. Apparently, Colin Mak has gone to jail a few times before for doing this same thing to other people in the past. From the message the officer left me, it looks like the Singapore police are going to put him in jail again for this. I feel so relieved! Nothing is set, but I think because he has a criminal record for doing this, the Singapore Police will act on this. Thank god! I really really hope this pans out and nothing happens to stop him from going to jail. Any word on your end from your friend, etc.?

Best,
Leandra \[145]

David wrote back:

That's great. My friend suggested that we just wait and see what the FBI did, and if they didn't respond, he would help escalate it. But it looks like the FBI and Singapore police are on the case, so no need to do more. If anything goes wrong, please let me know.
D[146]

My elation would be short-lived. The stalking continued unabated. Clearly, Mak wasn't in jail.

On May 20, 2007, I wrote David, frustrated:

David,

The FBI has done nothing. They said they would TRY to prosecute him, and I assumed that would happen, but nothing has happened yet and last time I spoke to the FBI they sounded doubtful. Singapore police never got back to me. Lawyers I spoke to said they can do nothing. Local police said there is nothing they can do either. I'm so desperate I'm thinking of writing Dateline or Nightline to do a story about this just to get this guy out of my life. Isn't what he is doing very illegal? Why is nothing being done? I don't understand!

You are the last resource I have. Now this stalker, (whom now it looks like there might be more than one person involved) is threatening and harassing the baritone I am singing with in Toledo Opera in addition to everyone else involved in my life he is harrassing. He is threatening physical harm to me by this Tuesday at my performance tomorrow and that he promises I will be physically harmed by if I don't write a signed letter to him. It is very scary as a woman to receive emails like this every day. I live in fear of even going anywhere alone. I am having a police man come to the performance tomorrow just to be safe. He told me his name was "Colin Mak" from Singapore, he told Tim his name is "Miggy Gulnara" from South America. He also claims he lives in New York. How do I know he doesn't live in the US?

He called my mom at 7AM this morning saying he will "strike". I am desperate. He is ruining so many things in my life including my relationships with people, relationships with companies, etc. PLEASE PLEASE help me. I was actually in DC today and wanted to call you but I lost your number when I switched phones. If you can call me I would greatly appreciate it. I know it is not your responsibility to help me, but I don't where else to turn now. If you can use your resources I would greatly appreciate it. I will be forwarding you one or two more of the many emails I have received in just the last 12 hours....I hope to hear from you soon.[147]

Revisiting Friends in High Places: National Intelligence Directorate

David responded May 21, 2007, the next day. He would see what his "friend" could find out.

Nels Nordquist was an official "very high up" in the National Intelligence Directorate, who wrote David:

My colleague Mike Tiffany will be in touch with the NYDP officer in Singapore. I forwarded him all the emails you sent me. If (Leandra) talks to anyone at NYPD, she should mention that we have discussed this case with Mike. He was one of their most senior officers, and he is widely and favorably known on the force. He said something needs to be done immediately. She definitely needs to be in touch with her contact at the FBI to let them know that she fears for her safety. She should ask what they are doing about this. The FBI should request that Singapore pull this guy's passport so he cannot travel. Also, she should ask that the FBI notify her should he attempt to enter the United States, and that he be put on a visa watch list. Mike also said she should, politely, ask for and record the name of the FBI agent to whom she talks about this matter. Please keep us informed.

As instructed, I did keep them informed, writing back to both David and Nels several hours later. In sum, the FBI was still ignoring me, although they had assigned me a new agent. I outline the efforts I made to contact them, below:

David and Nels,

First off, thank you so much for any help and advice regarding this psycho. I really appreciate that Mike Tiffany will be in touch with the NYPD in Singapore. Being that I am currently working in Toledo, Ohio I haven't had any contact with the NYPD for a few months now. Last time I spoke to the NYPD, I was in New York, and they advised me to just ignore it. One of the officers tried calling Mr Mak from my cell phone and it seemed to do nothing except provoke him more.

I agree that something definitely has to be done immediately. An opera company that my boyfriend previously worked for was contacted by Mr Mak this morning. They said they received an email ordering them to deliver a death threat to him and that it was "guaranteed" unless we give Mr Mak a signed letter of apology, he guarantees we will have broken bones by tomorrow. On another note, someone called Toledo Opera this morning asking where our schools performances will be tomorrow. We don't know if this is the stalker trying to locate me, or if it's even related. However, I will be going to the local police to protect myself for at least the next 24 hours.

I and my boyfriend have called the FBI multiple times over the weekend. We did tell the FBI that we fear for my safety. I haven't even heard back from the officer I have been assigned to for over 5 days now. The last time I spoke to him, he said he is waiting to hear back from the US Attorney's office and will get back to me when he knows anything. He also said he thinks the US attorney's office will probably decline to take this case further judging from his past experience.

My parents, my boyfriend and myself have all left him voice messages telling him how urgent this is. We have gotten no response lately. That officer is named Thomas Moore. Before him we were in contact with Alan Reichert and Michael Burglot with the FBI. They keep on giving us new officers. I did ask for them to pull his passport and/or flag him if he ever comes into the country. They said eventually, if they feel it is necessary, they will do that. Otherwise, they do nothing.

I have forwarded all of the latest emails to the FBI as I was told to do, and have not gotten even a response. It seems they are not going to take this seriously until I am physically harmed, or worse, and I am not going wait for that to happen.

Also, just to clarify, we do not know for sure that the stalker is even who he says he is. He said he was Colin Mak from Singapore when all this correspondence first started, but in other, later emails, he claimed he lived in NYC and called himself by different names, including "Miggy M""Mikky M" and "Miggy Gulnara." He also claimed he was from South America.

In the past, on a related note, we have also gotten emails from a "Jason Fitzpatrick" whom I looked up on the inter-net and found that he was a convict in the States. The stalker's alleged lawyer "Mona Hanson" from a Virginia cell phone also contacted us. It is possible that there is more than one person involved.

You both seem to be our only hope at this point. If he is who he says he is, maybe the Singapore Authorities can help put an end to the death threats and all the horrible life disruptions.

Thank you both so much again, and in advance for your help on this. My family, and Michael, and I greatly appreciate it. I will also forward you any emails I receive that I think might be relevant to help our case. .

I hope to hear from you very soon,
Leandra[148]

Nels responded:

"I will discuss this further with Mike and our colleague from FBI."[149]

The FBI never contacted me, nor did I hear back from Nels, the latter perhaps a result of a changing administration (with the accompanying personnel change).

The Feds' inaction and atrophy marked my first journey through government red tape, promises, and passing the buck. Despite the flurry of email-pushing among impressively credentialed authorities, I had gained no ground.

Ruminations on a System's Failure

The advice proffered by enigmatic government officials through David would be repeated by every law enforcement agency I'd contact over the next several years. It would prove ineffective and inaccurate, as evidenced by the thousands of emails, against the cyber attacks I suffered since then. True, I did not follow the advice to retreat and reinvent myself. That seemed utterly unrealistic for an artist whose living depended on her identity.

I appreciated David's efforts—he had no obligation toward me, yet he tried to help. However, law enforcement responses were, at best, lacking in imagination and, at worst, lazy and incompetent.

Years later, A.J., my law enforcement liaison, told me about a recent visit to the FBI Cybercrimes Unit in New York City. He had visited an area at headquarters internally referred to as "the bullpen." He got a general sense of recalcitrance—immovability, the status quo. He was appalled at the general sloth that surrounded him, food containers everywhere, no sense of urgency. This attitude carried over into his conversation with one surly agent, who tersely summarized the attitude I had felt from the beginning of my search for justice. Cybercrime victims? "They're all f**king nuts."

I suspected an even more insidious attitude, which prevailed in all of law enforcement, internationally and at home. Attractive women who had stalkers were asking for it. Why did I have to post sexy photos of myself online? Why were my big breasts so visible? What did I expect?

I often wondered how a federal agent would treat a family victim threatened with rape by nightstick, disfigurement with hot oil, or stabbing to death? Would they really have told their wives, daughters, and sisters to "fuggedaboutit"?

PHOTOGRAPHS

.RVARD UNIVERSITY POLICE DEPARTMENT

Criminal Investigation Unit
Phone (617) 495-1796
Fax (617) 495-7782
Emergency (617) 495-1212

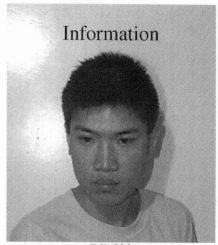

Colin Mak
address redacted Singapore
A/M, 5'7", 150 lbs., Brown Hair, Brown Eyes

The above individual was stopped at Lowell House on September 26, 2000 @ approximately 12:30 AM after a report of an individual sleeping in the basement. Subject has been given several trespass warnings and was arrested for trespassing on 9/12/00 by this department.

FYI

Above: Publically circulated notice from Harvard University Police regarding Colin as a trespasser on Campus in September 2000.

Above: Video surveillance apparently of Brian Asparro delivering flowers for Colin Mak at apartment of David and Adrienne Ramm.

this a true copy
of letter that
accompanied Flower Delivery

Silvestra...

If you received this-- it means my friend Brian from my Hong Kong days. He is a trusted American friend of mine.

I still love you with every bit of my heart. Lets forget about what happened in the past-- it is important for us to move forward. I think about you often even though I am so far away. I care about you deeply.

I am going to the Seychelles soon to complete my missons with the Royal Marines... it is an important and dangerous contract with the UK government. I am the commanding officer...

I guess in times like these-- it is so much more important for me to think about the ones I love and care about the most. I do not want to die without marrying you. I have never looked at or loved any other girl as much as I have for you.

Please email back soon to allay my fears.

Colin the warbird!
26th July-- Singapore.

Leandra Ramm
Apartment #231

Above: the letter enclosed with flower delivery.

Fax cover sheet above and content below.

Dear Adrienne Ramm

I pray this fax reaches you well.

Get your daughter Leandra Ramm to talk to me and I will not carry out the beating and blinding of Dustin Bear the saxophonist in due time.

I forgive your daughter Leandra for what she did-- but we need to talk.

I pray the time will not come when I have to confront you at Ballet East, break things, etc to ask you to ask Leandra to repent.

Leandra is very important to me and I love her a lot. I have spent a lot of money on her.

Thanks-- Leandra knows how to contact me-- get her to talk to me on google chat.

ALL MEDIA ATTACK: on the web, by email and here by a
threatening fax sent to Leandra's mother's employer.

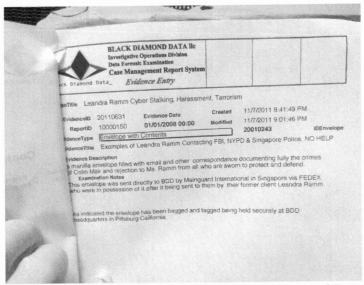

Above: Typical evidence entry from Black Diamond Data

Above: Letter and envelope sent to FBI, which had fingerprints matching Colin Mak.

Silvestro,

I am angry with you for I have not heard from you in nearly 2 weeks. Your voice and words revitalize me always. This I want you to know. I love you.

Just how are you doing on the ship I want to know. I am 100 percent jealous of you and 1000 percent wanting to make love to you in every luxury cabin on the ship in the middle of the ocean, totally oblivious to violent raging storms. May our cries of passion overwhelm them all!!! I have to make love to you soon my Silvestro. You drive me into the most pleasant states of wild, passionate frenzy.

I shall be having your most beautiful face in my hands, grabbing your breasts, holding you so tightly for fear of losing you. So tell me you love me and tell me you do care about me tell me my only love, that you want my very hard rod in your warm meaty Tell me you want to cover every golden drop of my sacred white elixir. I need to be loved by you. I need to marry you because every day without you is pure sexual torment I need to wake up every morning knowing I can give you wild, long and passionate lazy kisses my heart beg you to surrender.

love, your colin
26th March 2010

Above is a photograph of the letter that was enclosed in the envelope from which FBI crime labs matched fingerprints to Colin Mak.

bove: A.J. Fardella and Leandra Ramm at MLIALM premiere party at Desire Bar & Grill November 2012 in New York City.

Above: A.J. Fardella delivering lecture on Cybercrime at Contra Costa College March 2013 in San Ramon, California.

Above: Stalking A Diva authors Leandra Ramm and D. Rocca in London May 2013. Photo taken between filming Leandra's episode of **October Films'** "Obsessed" produced for **Investigation Discovery Network**.

Above: Leandra Ramm, D. Rocca and Alexis Bowater meeting in London May 2013

Above: Leandra Ramm in a modeling shot August 2010

Leandra Ramm

PART EIGHT
COPING

The Choice

In the later part of 2007, Colin's stalking and bullying was worsening, not, as various law and cyber experts had assured me, improving. I had been, as police continuously instructed, ignoring Colin since MWL's demand to cease and desist. For the previous two years, despite wearying efforts with local and federal law enforcement, despite filing police reports and all manner of paperwork from New York City to Singapore, I had gotten exactly nowhere.

As I said in my 2011 affidavit to Singapore, "Nobody was helping me and I was desperate so on or about July, 2007 I again began communicating with the perpetrator" (this was about 7 months after I stopped all interactions with him). I decided to communicate with the perpetrator because I knew that was the only way to get my life back since the law enforcement agencies I contacted were no help."[150]

I grimly assessed my situation. Colin had sent me hundreds of emails since the cease-and-desist letter, forcing MWL and me to exercise major, time consuming damage control measures. We couldn't keep up with Colin's attacks. To stave off Colin's constant attacks was a full-time job. I didn't have the time or the energy to spend on that endeavor, even if I'd wanted to. I had to work, not only to support myself but to keep myself in the game. I refused to let Colin defeat me with doubts.

It was time to make a decision between two terrible choices—continuing my détente with Colin, or caving to his demands that we resume our online communications. I explained it in my affidavit to the Secret Service and Singapore police,

"I decided to communicate with the perpetrator because I knew that was the only way to get my life back since the law enforcement agencies I contacted were no help."[151]

"I never wanted to communicate with him, but I felt it was my only choice. It was the only thing I could do to keep him from making things worse than what they already were. This prevented him from attacking me, my family, friends and colleagues and the places I worked. This allowed me to work again as a professional singer and feel somewhat at peace by not being stalked."[152]

Against all advice, I had chosen to wrest some control from Colin by initiating a dialogue.

Keeping Colin at Bay

It had been about six or seven months after I had initially stopped communicating with Colin, after the Austrian Schonbrunn debacle, and after MWL's[153] spectacular cease-and-desist" failure. The cease and desist aftermath was Colin's "scorched earth" policy. He would receive retribution for whatever wrongs he believed Michael Wade Lee, my family, or I had committed against him. Unless, somehow, I stopped him or slowed him down some.

So I used an approach, keeping Colin "at bay," which would be criticized by those same people who failed to help me (i.e., law enforcement and so-called experts in the field of cyber security). I did the *opposite* of what the "experts" told me to do. I called Colin.

There were two events which triggered the "at bay" period. First was Colin's email to the Martina Arroyo Foundation, for whom I was slated to play Dorabella in *Cosi' Fan Tutte*. I feared that this email put my role, my entire operatic career in jeopardy.

Dear Martina Arroyo Foundation

I am writing you from Wash, DC. I am an aviation consultant for the Pentagon.

I am Leandra Ramm's ex- sponsor of her education etc--quite recently Leandra Ramm engaged in serious wire fraud of 10 000 USD-- misusing my cash.
and she has engaged in threats, harassment of a Federally protected witness under the Witness Protection program with someone she has called her fiance-- that balless wimp Michael Wade Lee.
these are serious charges worth at least 1 year in a Federal prison time.

I am seeking an apology from Leandra Ramm on a signed letter for her abovementioned crimes.
I know she has a performance soon with you.
I look forward to seeing her at her performance.

I hope this matter can be settled--- I and my government agent friends do not want to meet Leandra Ramm after a performance with nightsticks to settle the matter extra-judicially.[154]

I had received far worse emails, but this one pushed me over the edge, the proverbial straw breaking the camel's back. I felt ready to check myself into an institution. I couldn't handle these threats anymore: the emails, voicemails, letters mailed to my parents' house. It just became too much. With law enforcement unable to help, I was at my ultimate low. I was desperate and depressed. I felt helpless.

Those feelings combined with my New York debut of a huge operatic role was a toxic mix. This was the biggest role I had yet to sing, and it was with a prestigious foundation to be performed with an orchestra in New York City. For him to attack me now was the worst possible timing. I had to do something.

The second trigger (chronologically speaking) was my bizarre subway encounter with Gregory Singer, also at the end of June 2007. Singer had called my stalker "harmless," and "nothing to worry about," emboldening me to contact Colin the next day.

In our vernacular, "at bay" or "to keep at bay" means to prevent someone from moving closer. Paradoxically, at bay also means "being unable to escape," derived from the 13th-century French: "abai," the hunted animal, the prey. For me, "at bay" was the opiate temporarily alleviating pain and giving me delusions of control over my predator. Initially, I convinced myself that I had turned the tables, and that *I* was in control of Colin, not the other way around.

The "at bay period" refers to that stretch of time between July 2007 and March 2010, when Colin and I had, in his words, "struck an accord." In 2007, I thought of "at bay" as the "prevent you from getting any closer" variety. In hindsight, I was more the hunted animal, unable to escape.

Détente—Sort Of

My approach was a little unorthodox, but it was honest, at least.

On or about June 29th, 2007, I called the perpetrator in Singapore and asked him what he wanted. He said he wanted to talk to me and demanded an apology. So I "apologized" even though of course there was nothing that I did wrong. I was very desperate to have peace again.

I was naïve in thinking that I would have peace. I hadn't had any type of calm or tranquility since before the *Anderson Cooper* broadcast at the end of 2005. In order to be left alone, I would have to make sacrifices, the first of which was to regularly contact my stalker. The law enforcement approach of ignoring Colin was failing miserably, and having no one to help me, I decided I would relinquish some freedom in exchange for a certain level of bargained-for "mercy."

"At bay" seemed to be the solution so that Colin wouldn't stalk me, terrorize me, threaten my coworkers and employers, and ruin my career.[155] At the beginning, I felt more empowered than I had in two years. At first, I "controlled" Colin's stalking with a status email "once every two weeks"[156] ... "saying something like 'hi, how's it going... how's the weather?'"[157]

Despite Colin's backing off, my anxiety increased. The problem was that I really didn't have any power. I had a truce with a virtual person who began demanding more than just emails. Eventually he wanted to have live "chat sessions." In my heart, I knew that this arrangement wouldn't last. I had to ask myself when the other shoe would drop.

Implicit in our arrangement was that I would play along, albeit passively, with my role in Colin's fantasy life— that of girlfriend. That concept disgusted me, but I was a trained performer. Surely, I could evade and fake my way through a chat session.

Contemplating Colin

Before our scheduled chats, about which Colin sadistically liked to remind and needle me, I couldn't help but contemplate with absolute disgust and horror where he was, his anticipation, and what he was possibly doing while I wrote to him. (He alluded to masturbating while on our chats together.)

I imagined a slight Asian man with a shaven head, mid-thirties by now, perspiring profusely while sitting riveted to a screen with a well-known picture of me garishly displayed. Maybe he was at his family home on Tanglin Road, where a woman's voice wafts through the door—his mother's, perhaps? I doubt that he would take well an imposition while he was about to enjoy a chat with me, nor would he be pleased by any reality that invaded his space. Maybe he was in an Internet café—often his place of choice, where he could enjoy some anonymity, but couldn't enjoy any personal intimacy pleasuring himself. I pushed those thoughts from my mind, focusing on the goal, which was to get through this nightmare, to act my way through it.

I knew what the consequences would be if I simply didn't show up at an appointed time. I imagine him beginning to stress out as our chat deadline approached, arriving early, doubting my loyalty, then the sweet relief of the chat line's telltale ping and with it my image coming to life.

Often, I thought up excuses in advance about how I could avoid communications with him. I was working and rehearsing, I was sick, I had a family emergency.

But one could only use these excuses so many times. Colin was relentless and would demand immediate rescheduling, threatening to "strike" my family, friends, the cruise ship where I performed.

Every Ten Days

As I swore in my affidavit to the United States Secret Service:

"Eventually, the perpetrator wanted IM[158] conversations every ten days. ...and I would always remind him not to stalk me or contact anyone else in my life since I knew that was his tendency when he didn't hear from me in a while."[159]

me: there are some things we need to talk about right now

warbird5k: okay

me: as in....you need to stop those horrible emails you send me and to my parents and my sister and to others
ok?
you promised before you wouldn't and you keep doing it

warbird5k: I don't know what to tell you Silvestra.[160]

And, in the same session:

me: and please stop sending emails to my parents that have threats in them and my sister

warbird5k: why aren't your parents even writing to me

me: it's not a good idea
your emails to them are inappropriate

warbird5k: its bad form
they are doing things in bad form
bad bad bad

me: ?
you are doing things in bad form! Sending my parents threats
how do you expect them to respond to those emails

warbird5k: no I asked in a friendly manner how they'd feel about me
will I see them in NYC or will I get only to see Birkles?
I am laughing

me: along with threats you sent them that
you have to be careful what you write in emails because people don't forget those..they remain in people's minds for a long time including mine
it affects people's opinion of you

In that same chat log, I try to convince Colin to lay off people outside of my family, including Michael Wade Lee, discussed below:

me: has he been in contact with you?

warbird5k: I told you he and I talked during the Olympic period
do you deny what he said?
you know what I am talking about here

me: yes, we were just friends. he was probably angry that you were harrassing him still so he said those things about me

warbird5k: ok

me: he probably never dreamed that by helping a friend out he would be harassed for years after
he was probably very upset and angry
now he doesn't talk to me

warbird5k: We Singaporeans have the Israeli doctrine in our blood having been friends with Israelis for so long
remember the movie-- MUNICH

me: no

warbird5k: my ex-girlfriend was a sabra-- an Israeli born Jew
Silvestra are u there

me: wait, we haven't finished talking about MWL....you really need to leave him alone. ok?[161]

me: I want you to promise me that you will not send any of those horrible emails, ok?
to any one!

Penalties for Non-Compliance

If I missed a chat date with Colin, he retaliated in emails, threatening great bodily harm to me, my family, friends, and work contacts. He also telephoned me or my parents constantly, leaving hundreds of messages on our answering machines. In his messages to me, regardless of how they began, he ended the call with an automaton-like, "I love you very much." It made me sick to have to listen to these, but I knew they were evidence in my criminal cases, so I recorded them.

Most of the time, I would ignore the phone calls. It was a fine line, because if I remained incommunicado for too long, "he sent me death threats or something similar."[162] Because I was in fear for my life, I would answer the phone, hoping to prevent those threats from becoming real.[163]

Tit for Tat—Controlling Chat

In exchange for non-harassment, Colin began demanding more than idle chatter. My response was passive-aggressive, to let him rant and rave, while steering the conversation away from inappropriate sexual communications, and receiving assurances from him that he would cease harmful emails. It was an exercise in diplomacy.

me: I want you to promise me that you will not send any of those horrible emails, ok?
to anyone!

warbird5k: ok I promise. you must promise to meet me at JFK
is it okay?
Silvestra you didn't let me finish, I keep thinking about sex with you that's why I became angry when I felt snubbed.

me: well I should go now.

warbird5k: wow
that was great. and I am being sarcastic
so you understand?

me: that's inappropriate to say[164]

As our chats progressed, Colin became bolder, becoming "more demanding" and "saying he loved me and wanted to marry me."[165] I sidestepped those conversations, dubbing them "inappropriate" and off limits.

By 2010, I was losing control. We still "met" for our Internet chats, but he was stalking—in direct violation of our "accord." In the chat log below, I referred to threatening emails he had just sent.

me: I just read them and was wondering what was going on with you? are you ok?

warbird5k: I am
just that I was afraid you'd betray me
can u understand?

me: no I can't understand to be honest. I can understand if you wrote to me personally and asked me and talked to me, but why did you write to all those people? It's weird

warbird5k: I had to protect myself

me: you owe me a big apology because you promised me you wouldn't send me any threats and you did. The title of your email was "warning"...if that's not a threat then what is?[166]

Shortly before Valentine's Day 2010 began a barrage of threats, despite our having "chatted" just a few days previously. Not believing my claim that the Internet was down, he wrote:

"internet failure will not be a valid excuse
I hope to get a reply from you on 14th February.
Hey-- I got a fantastic idea-- why not break contact from me for several weeks to months like you did to me in HK? Why? Don't you dare to do this? Is it because you fear MWL …. will be killed?
--
Colin M, Molto Allegro!

~~ "So Long As The Human Spirit Thrives On This Planet, Music In Some Living Form Will Accompany And Sustain It And Give It Expressive Meaning." Aaron Copland ~~[167]

Gifts and Letters

From February 2006 until December 2006 and from July 2007 until March 2010, the perpetrator sent me gifts in the mail and love letters from Singapore. This entire period, I was terrified and felt very abused.[168] Most were sent during the "at bay" times, when I was communicating with Colin, thereby trying to keep him in my sights in order to control him.

For five years, Colin talked about and sent me gifts and letters, in the mail and through his minions. On average, I received gifts (at my parents' home in New York) about once every two or three months.

His gifts became increasingly personal--perfume delivered by messenger Gregory Singer at the violin shop audition, Chinese shoes (he managed to get my shoe size from me during a chat session), gold designer UK flats, a gold-plated necklace with a pearl, actually quite beautiful, and, eventually, lingerie.

Darling Silvestra...
You say you don't give out intimate sizes...!
But based on your vital measurements-- don't you think if I show it to the salesgirl in La Senza she can tell me your size? ;)????

Quick! Give me the colors you want and the items you want... I am outside the shop now -- 2 metres away because the computer lounge is right here... I will go to the shop next week again...

They have red, pink, amethyst, sky blue, azure, black, blue and white checks, black and white checks, nude colors, baby dolls, pale yellow with small floral print bras...

Why is it that I am thinking about sex right now again????? Let me see-- I'll get you a baby doll, a bra and panty set and nude colored stockings.. or do you want black thigh high stockings... plus a boy leg or two?

Well I had better not talk about that-- even I feel uncomfortable... ;) [169]

He also sent me a red, silk Chinese wedding dress.

I never returned gifts ... just kept most of them in a collection and others I threw out to get rid of him and the memory of him. I admit that I tried on some of these items. I'm not sure why. Maybe I wanted something beautiful to justify the ugliness wrought by my predator. Maybe I was following his directions because I didn't have a choice. His imaginary world was increasingly pervading my everyday reality, blurring the boundaries between them.

Later, the true purpose behind my keeping them occurred to me—they were the means to my end of getting this creep arrested; they were the type of proof that law enforcement couldn't ignore.

Like the emails, chat logs, and phone recordings, I would eventually turn them over to my law enforcement liaison, A.J. Fardella, who "bagged and tagged" them as evidence to be submitted to Singapore police. Colin's "love" letters, usually from Singapore hotel stationery, met the same fate. In fact, all these pieces of hard evidence became the subject of ensuing police forensic investigations, including fingerprinting and black lighting.

Flower Delivery

Until 2010, the only gift I received via courier were those odd Chanel perfume testers delivered by Gregory Singer in 2007, after that surreal audition at his violin shop. That was at the beginning of Colin's stalking and, unlike the delivery I was to receive 3 years later, it was not at my home.

In July 2010, it had been several months after I had ceased "at bay" and all further communications with my stalker. Refusing to be ignored, Colin enlisted minion Brian Asparro, the one with impeccable credentials, who should have known the nefarious nature of what he was about to do, to hand-deliver a bouquet of pink flowers to my parents' home.

My mother Adrienne, the eternal optimist, had suggested we put them in a vase because they were pretty. I vehemently refused to let that poisoned energy reside in our home. Pretty or not, they belonged in the garbage.

My father bolted out of our building, unsuccessfully chasing after the Asparro, the deliveryman, whose image was caught on videotape. I reluctantly contacted NYPD. Predictably, their advice was to ignore what was happening to me.

Unlike the other gifts, the flower delivery was a message from my stalker, less to woo than to highlight my vulnerability. I wrote in my affidavit to the Secret Service:

"I am scared for my life. I am scared for my family, friends and colleagues' lives. My reputation has been ruined and my career has been very much affected because of this. I live in fear, anxiety and turmoil because of the stalking and cyber-terrorism. I have psychological long-term damage because of the extortion, cyber-terrorism and the effect this has had on my relationships, career and life. [170]

Survival Mode: Stockholm Syndrome

Stockholm syndrome refers to a group of psychological symptoms that occur in some persons in a captive or hostage situation.[171] The term takes its name from a bank robbery in Stockholm, Sweden, in August 1973. The robber took four bank employees into the vault with him and kept them hostage for 131 hours. After the robber released the three women and a man, they appeared to have formed a paradoxical relationship with their captor, concluding that the police were their enemy and forming positive feelings toward the bank robber. The term has been used to describe Patty Hearst's reaction to her kidnapping in 1974, as well as Elizabeth Smart's in 2002.

People who often feel helpless in other stressful life situations, or are willing to do anything in order to survive, seem to be more susceptible to developing Stockholm syndrome if they are taken hostage.

I was not kidnapped, nor did I ever meet Colin. So I obviously did not suffer from Stockholm syndrome, technically speaking. I did, however share some of the victim attributes, the most prevalent being that I had entered my "at bay" relationship, believing that I would do anything in order to survive. When I contacted Colin in summer 2007, I felt it was my only choice.

I also felt an enormous sense of gratitude toward Colin for giving me the opportunity to take this route against his stalking. I was grateful for his agreement not to terrorize my employers, my family, friends, even former friends, and myself.

The opera world had ingrained in me gratefulness for any opportunity, which set the stage for allowing Colin into my life at the beginning. Now I had extrapolated this appreciativeness to masochism. I saw an "opportunity" to stop him from committing crimes against me. Looking back, I'm appalled at the sickness of my mindset, but forgive myself. After all, I was in survival mode.

Riding it Out

It was frustrating to Colin when I didn't respond to his constant incitement with fear and groveling. So he ridiculed my calmness and attributed it to my Buddhism, which he also ridiculed. Colin was a self-professed Christian who practiced his religion in an affluent Singaporean Chinese Christian church, another irony, given his hateful and unforgiving behavior.

But really, it was less the Buddhism that sustained me than a survival technique. I couldn't allow myself to be sucked into his reality by showing anger and lack of control.

It was evident I couldn't fight Colin on his cyber turf. So, my choices were to appease him or ignore him. I paid a high price for both approaches. In either case, I had to employ meditative-type techniques, focusing on the present and not dwelling on the misery he was intent on inflicting; that would surely cause me to wallow in self-pity.

During the at bay period, Colin still controlled and stalked me, but he wasn't threatening my life, job, and the lives and jobs of my work associates and friends. But I suffered from terrible anxiety and feeling trapped; a slave to my stalker. My fear was very much alive; it had just morphed from the panic of undoing harm to the anxiety about what would happen if I didn't comply with his strict rules. I knew if I didn't communicate every ten days, he would do something awful and there was still no guarantee that he wouldn't. I was dealing with a madman. And because he was increasingly "in love" with me, I was scared he would follow through on his threats to enter my physical life, even end it.

Ultimately, my sense of dignity prevailed over the illusory safety net of "at bay." This was no way to live a life—in constant turmoil about "what if's," while suffering the humiliation and expense of humoring a man I detested.

"At Bay" was a failure; it hadn't yielded the tranquility nor the control I'd expected. It was time for a change.

PART NINE
ENOUGH! THE END OF AT BAY

Prelude to Freedom

"Those who sacrifice liberty for security deserve neither."....Ben Franklin

In 2010, I was one of four lead singers, two men and two women, featured on a cruise ship, travelling the routes of Caribbean pirates in a vessel the size of a small metropolis. I had agreed to chat with Colin every ten days. I was not keeping my end of the bargain. One of the reasons I went on the cruise ship was to escape. I thought that by escaping land, I would escape Colin. I was wrong, as Colin followed me on a virtual plane—everywhere.

At 19 cents per minute, the ship's Internet fees were exorbitant as was any communication, in or out, while we were at sea. I didn't contact my agents or my family from the ship, waiting until we entered port, where I could use an Internet café. And yet, as my then-boyfriend Dustin had pointed out, I was spending hundreds of dollars on dreaded, awful conversations with Colin. The cruel irony of my situation was hitting me hard.

Colin was getting fed up with my increasing excuses for missing our chat dates; of having to work, lack of ship's Internet, illness, and family issues.

By March, 2010, I was certain that even if I'd kept all our appointments, our "accord" was no longer effective—Colin wanted more and I wanted out. Deep down inside, although I was afraid to admit it, I knew that the terms of "at bay" were about to change.

Crescendo

At the beginning of March, 2010, my stalker was becoming more demanding, and I was less willing to play the "at bay" game anymore.

Claiming he was on the ship, Colin was relentless, craving more attention and acting more sexually crazed by the minute.

From: Colin M warbird5k☐
To: Silvestra
March 3, 2010 3:28 AM

I am still on a sexual high and will be till I get to talk to you.
Thursday can we talk?
--

Colin M, Molto Allegro!
~~ "So Long As The Human Spirit Thrives On This Planet, Music In Some Living Form Will Accompany And Sustain It And Give It Expressive Meaning." Aaron Copland ~~

and,

From: Colin M warbird5k☐
Date: Thu, Mar 11, 2010 at 4:22 AM
Subject:
To: Leandra Ramm leandraramm
Silvestra

what are you wearing today for both intimates and outerwear?
is it something exciting?
--

Colin M, Molto Allegro

From: Colin M warbird5k☐
Date: Thu, Mar 11, 2010 at 5:22 AM
Subject:
To: Leandra Ramm leandraramm

Leandra
can you promise me you are really a virgin?
thats good to know... ;)
I may having too many sexual fantasies about you of late and need to put myself deeply into you.

Soon after, he wrote:

From: Colin M warbird5k ☐
Date: Sat, Mar 13, 2010 at 5:20 AM
Subject:
To: Leandra Ramm leandraramm

I am on a sexual high again
can we talk soon darling
please... I need you.
its getting unbearable.
I plan to get on the ship-- when its starting towards Europe...
lets talk soon
I have an erection now because the weather is good again and I am happy.

And:

From: Colin M warbird5k ☐
Date: Sun, Mar 14, 2010 at 5:50 AM
Subject:
To: Leandra Ramm leandraramm

Silvestra
I need sex soon--- but not before I get married to you and ram you night after
night against the ceiling, on the kitchen table, the divan, bed, bathroom and
the chandeliers.
I will probably leave semen trails all about the house-- visible only by UV
blacklight... ;)
Colin M, Molto Allegro!

~~ "So Long As The Human Spirit Thrives On This Planet, Music In Some Living
Form Will Accompany And Sustain It And Give It Expressive Meaning." Aaron
Copland ~~

Clearly, the efficacy of keeping Colin "at bay" was waning,
and I realized that by this time he actually believed we were
in a relationship, that we were on our way to getting
married, and he was going to live with me in New York. For
me, "at bay" was a ticket to survival, a hard-fought
negotiation for minimal peace of mind. For him, it was a
relationship that was moving forward. I realized this, and
knew I was in way over my head. You can't reason with a
crazy person. I was becoming way too important to him
and realized "at bay" was backfiring.

220

Colin was beginning to get angry again and he was erratic. His emails changed course, moving from sexually predatory to hateful stalker mode, then back again. I didn't know which one was more disturbing; both sickened me:

From: Colin M
<warbird5k>□□□
□□
Date: Wed, Mar 17, 2010 at 12:50 AM
Subject: list of easy things you have refused to do for me-- requests made in the last 2 years
To: Leandra Ramm <leandraramm>

#1 refusal to sing for me over the phone (request made in 2007 October)
#2 refusal to take a picture of Birkles to send to me (request made since April 2009)
#3 refusal to send Linn or Ying Tan a package (request made since December 2009)
#4 refusal to ask your parents to send me just an email (request made since June 2009)
#5 refusal to ask MWL to send me an apology (or even Eryn Pola)
#6 refusal to tell me when you signed the contract to board the Cruise Ship. (asked for since June 2009, but not indicated, now I am asked by you to board that expensive ship which I am going to do)

I would like to keep a score of things Silvestra so it would indicate which areas we are even and which ones we are not.

A small problem, I learnt in an aviation magazine last night-- is actually a bigger problem struggling to get out.
All the requests cost you nothing. You know what to do and what will happen if you don't.
--
Colin M, Molto Allegro!

~~ "So Long As The Human Spirit Thrives On This Planet, Music In Some Living Form Will Accompany And Sustain It And Give It Expressive Meaning." Aaron Copland ~~

and,

Colin M <warbird5k>
where are you????????????? I am close to losing myself in you!!!
March 25, 2010 11:37 PM

Simultaneously, Colin was sending hundreds of other emails to me from different email addresses. I was an anxiety-ridden, neurotic mess.

Mutiny Musings

The Celebrity Equinox cruise ship where I performed the Winter and Spring of 2010 was, at the end of March, sailing somewhere in the Caribbean (St. Thomas—St. Kitts—Barbados—Dominica—St. Maarten).

I was relaxing after my performance, taking in a jazz set. Dustin was playing the saxophone. In the back of my mind, I knew that I had a chat date with Colin at nine sharp.

I ordered two glasses of wine and felt a bit tipsy, a little more rebellious than usual. I kept looking at my watch, counting the minutes until I would have to leave my boyfriend for my date with Colin. I suddenly realized how ridiculous it was for me to live like this—imprisoned and overpowered by a two-dimensional personality whom I only knew through machines.

At that moment, I decided not to "meet" Colin at nine, although I knew what the consequences would be. After our missed appointment and my enjoyable evening, I went back to my tiny, windowless cabin on the ship (quite different from the beautiful guest area I was just in); more than two hours later. Even in my tipsy state, curiosity got the best of me. I logged on to the Internet and checked my email. There were five threatening emails from Colin, copying others. That tipsy feeling at once left my body. I have never sobered up so quickly. Within seconds, my heart started to race and the blood pumped through my body. I discovered the consequences of my actions and they weren't pretty. I thought how crazy it was that I was living my life like this—if you could call this living.

Dustin had told me to stop "at bay." It wasn't working; it was draining and stress-inducing. I was paying an outrageous amount of money to do something I detested and dreaded. (At 19 cents per minute, cruise line rates are exorbitant; the crew avoided them and would swap files on thumb drives, rather than pay for email access.)

I felt, though, that ignoring Colin was worse—the threats would multiply and he would escalate. In Dustin's eyes, Colin and I shared the same major weakness—the need to be in control. Dustin wanted me to just let go. Dustin couldn't accept this other man in my life, a detested predator, no less, and threatened that if I kept communicating with Colin, he was out.

The choice was clear: It was either Dustin or Colin.

Convincing Dustin Bear

I met Dustin Bear, my boyfriend since 2009, in a Turkish café while working on the same Mediterranean cruise. A saxophonist in the ship's orchestra, Dustin learned to play from his grandfather. He began performing at eight and was a professional by thirteen. Dustin hailed from Iowa and Kentucky, combining southern chivalry with strong Midwestern values. His family was Rockwellian, compared to my bohemian, Jewish, Buddhist, science-fiction-inspiring clan. For me, it was love at first sight.

Initially, like everyone else, Dustin's advice was to ignore Colin; he differed in that he wanted to be involved, asking me to forward him Colin's emails.

I had been down this road before. Ignoring Colin didn't work. I was frustrated because I knew better. It felt like a Michael Wade Lee déjà vu.

Dustin,

I just forwarded you a sampling of emails from March. He sent others but I think I sent you the most relevant to the problem. He emails me everyday, talks about sexual things more and more and is very verbally abusive. I know, I know I know that you want me to just not read it and forward everything to you. I just wish you could feel what it's like in my shoes to be the one being attacked by him. It's so hard to just "ignore". When someone tries to ruin your life and career, it's hard to just pretend it's not happening. That's why I want to do something. I want your help. I can't just ignore him forever. He says he is coming on the ship, it's obviously a bluff, but still is frustrating.

I will come to a compromise with you....it's March 15th today.. I will ignore and send you everything from today until March 31st. (to start). You will see the emails will become more and more crazy, abusive and threatening each day I ignore. He will start contacting other people in about a week from now trying to ruin my reputation. I want to show you what I go through. I really honestly in my heart believe we need to tell him to f**k off or else he will keep thinking it's ok to keep doing what he's doing. I'm ready to tell him get out of my life. If you can help, that be great.

love,
L [172]

A week later, I was at my breaking point. I had lost my "A-Pass," a ship document required for disembarking. I needed to get off the ship, take my mind off Colin.

Dustin,

i can not sleep...it's 3:30am. I had to come back to my room. I couldn't even find my apass..its somewhere in your room. If you check your email before you leave for scuba in the morning, please keep your door a crack open so that I can find my apass and get off the ship tomorrow.

I am just so upset about this stalker problem. I HATE it when it gets into level 2. You will see, I can't sleep at night, I stress out, check my email all the time. Talk about quality of life, it will go down the tube! I really am doubting our plan of ignoring him. Did you see the emails he just sent? It will only get worse and worse and worse. I really don't think I can handle it.[173]

I provoked Dustin: If you're my boyfriend, then why don't you defend me against him? Looking back, I realize I was putting unfair pressure on Dustin, testing him. Was I worth the pain of going to war with Colin? Dustin thought so and suggested that we write Colin a letter, together.

Removing the Shackles

I was convinced that short of Colin's arrest and incarceration, there were only two ways the stalking would end—either by his death, or mine. So, as I said in my affidavit to the United States Secret Service, "On March 29, 2010, I sent the perpetrator a cease and desist letter and haven't responded or communicated to him in any way since and never plan to again."[174]

My final communication to Colin was the most liberating moment in my life. It was not spontaneous, but carefully planned. I had prepared two versions[175] and had consulted with my parents and Dustin. Finally, I felt ready to end this sick dynamic once and for all. Perhaps sensing the inevitable ending, Colin preempted my final letter with his own apology email.

Silvestra...
FORGIVE ME. I need your forgiveness here because I have done you very very very much wrong. I am and was afraid of losing you. I don't want to lose you! Please understand I admit my fault here and did not put you in consideration. I know I have said it before but I am asking for your grace and forgiveness again.
I regret my threatening actions and hurtful words--- please give me another chance. Yes, I was wrong. Totally wrong. I am not a stalker, harasser etc. I am not crazy but rather I am crazy and jealous about you. I just want to be with you and have a proper relationship! Lets talk this over on the ship....! I got so jealous when I saw so many guys on your account saying that they found you attractive etc.... sorry I got crazy. Yes I was stupid to say h

I want you to know that no matter how angry I was with you--- all the while you have meant so much to me! Even when I thought you were with MWL etc That was the heartbreaking part that left me crying in bed several nights! So many nights I dreamt of a reconciliation but did not know how to do this. I cried and cried!

I don't want things to fall apart especially after we have gone this far. I had opportunities for other beautiful women but all along I thought you were most beautiful to me!!! Physically as well as in the heart.

I do not want to move on because you mean the world to me. I cannot imagine you in the arms of another man. It makes me both angry and sad.

Silvestra... please... can we talk soon. Please... please... I don't want to ever quarrel with you again and promise I will be more understanding. Please forgive me for my impatience and lack of understanding here. I know I sinned against you.

I think you were probably very busy thats why an email could not be sent by you. I know you had to prepare for that blog interview... it was a great interview.

Please don't be angry anymore with me. I am not looking at any other girl BUT YOU! Listen--- I am wrong here for making demands etc.

However bad I am-- please don't leave me. I know you are angry with me and I am wrong here. I totally regret things because I realize I still need you. I love you very much.

I hope you are well and I know you will always be. I care very deeply about you please can we talk? I need you please write back and tell me how you feel. I have been inconsiderate and selfish to a beautiful girl like you. Can you please not be angry anymore with me?
--
Colin M, Molto Allegro! [176]

Instead, I used his desperate apology as the opening I needed to end this thing. I took it.

At 3:49 AM, in an email to warbird5k, miggymiggy, and spicekits, I wrote:

Colin Mak Yew Loong,

So, I guess you've been waiting on some communication from me. Well, here's what you asked for. This is the last email you will ever receive from me. I will not speak with you anymore. I will NOT be communicating with you anymore in any way. Communication with you is a waste of my time and I am choosing to move on in my life. I will NOT be reading your emails or communicating with you in any way. Get the Point? You are a stalker, a harasser, an international criminal and I want NOTHING to do with you. I do not care about your threats and sending them is just a waste of time. Any email from you is automatically deleted from my accounts. I and everyone else can see by your emails that you are crazy, mentally ill, obsessed with me and stalking me. I am DONE with you. We never were in a relationship and we NEVER will be. I am moving on with my life and you should too. Game Over. GOODBYE!

Leandra Ramm

Although I knew there would be major repercussions, I already felt better. Now, I vowed to myself, I would NEVER go back to being subjugated and enslaved by Colin, no matter what the consequences. At some point, I'd have to contend with the years and years of psychological and sexual abuse, insults, degradation, and objectification experienced under his oppressive rule. But for now, I'd begun my recovery.

With freedom came an unshakable confidence. Where before I felt beaten down, I now looked at failure in law enforcement, or the system generally, as just another opportunity to fight harder. I would need that confidence and strength.

By asserting myself, I had initiated the ultimate battle to put Colin away. Like a cornered, panicked animal, Colin would fight harder and dirtier than ever to maintain his power over me. I suspected that the worst was yet to come.

I was right.

PART TEN
STALKING ESCALATION 2010

Element of Surprise

Colin was unfazed by my declaration of independence. He was used to lapses in communication from me, and to my "cease-and-desist" demands. Historically, they were all unsuccessful.

I knew that once Colin learned of Dustin Bear, his terrorism would escalate; Colin's approach toward my boyfriends (or those he deemed possible romantic competition) was "take no prisoners." Colin's end game was to vanquish anyone who could vie for my affections. Doubtless, Colin's confidence would be shaken when he realized that he had been pursuing the wrong man, Michael Wade Lee, for several years. Desperation would breed more hate mail. I had warned Dustin that he would be a target.

True to form, though, when I ended communications with Colin, Dustin didn't flinch. He had studied Colin, and conceived a plan of attack. He was ready.

Colin, on the other hand, did not yet know of Dustin. The element of surprise was on our side.

The Plan

Dustin was intent on ridding both of us of Colin's scourge. He explained his strategy in an email to my agency Scarlett Entertainment's Rebecca Marks, who had recently been harassed by "Frank Tobias," another of Colin's aliases.

"Frank" had written Becky about me, threatening to have me "beaten up" and thrown off the cruise ship. He closed the email, "F**k you Becky."[177]

Several hours later, Becky wrote to Dustin, asking him how to block Colin's emails. She wrote, "They are coming from different addresses. I'm not sure if I should report this to anyone?"[178]

Dustin responded with an outline of his plan to fight Colin and some suggestions on how Becky could block emails.

Becky,

Hi how are you? Nice to meet you and thank you for contacting me as I will be more than happy to help you. You are more than welcome to send any future emails to me as I keep everything on record and compile information for future use. This will be helpful evidence in prosecuting this guy. I know these emails can be disturbing but please don't fear, Leandra is in good hands and the stalker is not on the ship nor has ever been even close to being in contact with Leandra. I advise her not to read the emails as the content can sometimes get in her head. This is the stalkers only weapon; words.

My mission is to get him completely banned from using any email server like Hotmail, Gmail, Me, Yahoo…etc., and if possible use the email below and other evidence against him when the time arises. I don't see the need to go out of your way and report this matter to anyone however, you can if you wish and if your help is needed in the future, Leandra or I or the authorities will contact you. Thank you again for your support.

As to block the emails I will be more than happy to help. So I suggest this: contact the manager or server company hosting your "scarlettentertainment" domain name. Whoever manages this will be able to but a blacklist on this email(s), and any other emails associated with a similar name or phrase. If you host your own website yourself and control the server yourself; login into your hosting page online, go to your email preferences (this may be different depending on the host) and blacklist email addresses there. If this is all confusing please let me know and I will do my best to be at your service.

My future suggestion is to handle this kind of situation like handling spam or mass advertisement emails: try not to read the emails if they are "bothering you", forward them to me or Leandra (I get everything she gets anyway) and we will keep it on file for possible future use in prosecution, and set up a block with your email server. If the stalker cannot reach anyone, is not being communicated with, is blocked, and he keeps hitting "walls", he will give up and move on. Of course action can and most likely will be taken against him, and that is being taken care of now.

I hope this helps. Leandra enjoys working with you and appreciates your support with this "not so threatening" but rather annoying idiot.

Thank you and keep in touch if you have anymore questions or concerns.

Cheers![179]

The Hunter

Dustin began his counterattack on May 21, 2010 with an email to Colin:

"Are you looking for a Leandra Ramm?"[180]

Colin, clearly not used to being on the receiving end of an email chain, backs down, using a different ploy, somewhat successful with Tim Hill of seeking a sympathetic ear:

On 5/22/10 8:36 AM, "Colin M" warbird5k wrote:

Dear Dustin
I don't think you should get involved.
Why are you emailing me? Will your saxophone help me in this regard?
I have been hurt enough already.
I am looking for peace.

Attempting to weasel more distance between him and Dustin, Colin writes an obsequious "explanation" a few hours later:

On 5/22/10 11:55 AM, "Colin M" warbird5k wrote:

Dear Dustin

I know you were writing me just as you and Leandra were logging on to the internet. She was probably telling you to write to me and its odd that she is asking to speak to me through you! Thanks for being polite!

I leave in a few days soon as I can see my trip is going nowhere. I had hoped to stay longer and enjoy time and dinners with Leandra but I understand that in life a lot of disappointments come and go. I had hoped to see Leandra as she promised and discussed with me a few months ago.

But its okay-- I understand her hesitation. I have spent a lot of money on this trip. No pressure. Never mind. If things change she can always email me to meet at the Murano restaurant. But again I love and respect Leandra and her wishes.

Thanks a lot and God bless Leandra Ramm--- her singing is great and it matches the angels in their glory.
I pray also that you will enjoy your time in Miami when you get back to the USA.

Now it was Dustin's turn. He was brilliant.

On Sat, May 22, 2010 at 11:17 AM,
Dustin Bear bearsax wrote:

Colin M,

Get involved? Are you afraid of me? Let me tell you something. I will always get involved when those I respect, love and care about are being hurt, damaged, harassed, stalked, intimidated, etc. Furthermore, no one has to tell me what to do or what to say when it comes to protecting my own. I am my own person, my actions are my own, and so is my love *and* my wrath.

Don't give me your pity party, "oh I'm hurt enough already" crap. You're not fooling me. Are you calling me an idiot? Do you think I don't understand who you really are what you're doing?

Anybody can figure out you have to log on to the to use it. Anybody can figure out that ships use satellite internet, and everyone knows you're not on this ship, nor are you even close to it or Leandra. I know you're halfway around the world sitting behind some random computer pretending to be somewhere you're not. Are you trying to be clever?

If you're looking for peace you can stop contacting Leandra, her friends, her family and anyone else associated with her. If you want respect, stop contacting others about her on your behalf posing to be someone who represents her in any way. If you want to show you are a loving person, you can stop spreading your lies involving her, and keep your stalking, harassing, intimidating, unwanted and less than civilized thoughts and actions to yourself involving her and anyone and anything associated with her. You do this and you'll have your peace. You understand what I'm saying? Are you listening to every word I'm typing?

Yes, God bless Leandra Ramm. Her singing *is* god's gift to the earth and you'd better pray I don't come and you myself if you continue to try and ruin her life any further. You mess with her, you mess with me. Got it?

You've got some choices to make now and I don't give out second chances.

Dustin Bear

Colin relents further, looking weak and pathetic:

On Sat, May 22, 2010 at 5:05 PM, Colin M warbird5k wrote:

Dustin

I am not afraid of you. I have been supporting Leandra all these years and will not be shortchanged.

I am on the ship.
If you are looking for a fight-- I can handle it.
Where do you want to meet me on the ship.

I do not want to call Linn records to stop negotiation with regards to the Cd recording just like I have done with my friend's label before.

Why is Leandra doing this?
I did the previous things mentioned because i was shortchanged.
thats all.

Leandra-- I am looking for peace and resolution.
I want resolution and justice.

Dustin-- do you know the facts of our story?

Unable to wait, he writes Dustin the next day:

On 5/23/10 1:05 PM, "Colin M" warbird5k wrote:

dear Dustin

HI again

I am going to prove to you I am serious about what was discussed today by sending you a hardcopy-- I will ask my secretary in Sweden to do it immediately.

<Dustin's parents' address redacted>

I am determined to reconcile with Leandra its up to her.

She is VERY VERY important to me and nothing else matters. There is no need to reply to me as I consider you and I to be at peace already. Thanks for your understanding.

- Forwarded message ----------
From: *Dustin Bear* <bearsax>
Date: Mon, May 24, 2010 at 7:40 AM
Subject: Re: Leandra Ramm
To: Colin M <warbird5k>

Colin,

As long as you continue to send correspondence and communicate, your trespassing in a place where you're not wanted. Reply to you? You're replying to me dickhead.

Looks like you got an address. "/Oh nooooo..... I'm soooo scared. I'm shivering in the corner now. Please don't hurt me."/ F**K YOU BITCH! You

236

think you can get into my head? You think you can mess with me? Too bad, so sad, 'cause it ain't gonna work Mother F**ker.

Leandra's already made up her mind. I know you got her email. You're not listening to her wishes and that pisses me off. You disrespect her and that pisses me off. You challenge her and think you can do what you want with her? Now you've f**king gone too far ass swab. You've sacrificed your desires for my wrath. Not a smart move.

She is very very important to you? What about what's important to her?

Let me tell you what's important to her. What's important to her is her freedom of having you out of her life because that's what she has told you time and time again. I can see that her words are not getting across to you and that's not right that you continue to disregard the one you say you care about. That's not love. That's selfishness. I will defend her honor out of real love and defend her desires as I share the same.

I don't care what you consider because you're only considering for yourself. However, consider this. You're being hunted. Change your ways and I'll back off. As of now, you're just giving me more of a reason to keep making your life less than peaceful.

I know your games, I know your past, I know what pisses you off, and I know you think you can get everything you want. You have an address on

me? So what! I've got nothing to to hide. You however have been hiding your whole f**king life. You wanna know what it's from? It's the million dollar question!

Out of all the things you avoid, fear, and hide from the most in life, it's yourself.

You're insecure because you can't find happiness within yourself. You've always thought it came from someone else. Wake up buddy. It's even deeply rooted in your own culture. To find true happiness all you have to do is look within. This is obviously not something you do enough of because right now you're still taking more time away from the one person who should be the most important in your life. You.

I'm happy. Leandra's happy. The whole world is happy but yet you continue to be pissed off because you blame your problems on everyone else. Take some f**king responsibility for yourself and your actions and what you say. You're not a child anymore so stop acting like one. Grow up Mother F**ker.

The Hunter

As a last resort, Colin forwarded the email chain, which he described as "vulgarities from Dustin" to my parents and sister, seeking their sympathy.

Colin had a formidable adversary in Dustin, who had clearly asserted his dominance in this first battle. And the next.

Dustin was on fire!

Turnabout is Fair Play

Dustin turned the tables on Colin, proclaiming himself "The Hunter," and Colin, simply, "Stalker." In creating this allegorical dynamic, Dustin had effectuated a power shift.

From: Dustin Bear bearsax
Subject: Waiting for me?
Date: May 26, 2010 11:17:40 AM EDT
To: warbird5k

Here I come Stalker!

The Hunter

In response, Colin, impersonating a colleague of mine, writes a self-serving "good bye" letter to me:

-----Original Message-----
From: Carina Scott carinascott.scott51 To: leandraramm
Cc: debkarpel; becky; michaelwadelee
Sent: Mon, May 24, 2010 10:34 pm
Subject: Fwd: Bye forever Leandra

Leandra
I have to tell your friends I am pulling out of your circle. I got the emails above from the email lists that Colin has been sending and I guess this ends our friendship.
Goodbye.

But Dustin would not tolerate this thinly veiled role-playing:

On 5/25/10 5:59 PM, "Dustin Bear" bearsax wrote:

No I know for sure you know the very evil you portray. You cannot hide behind others for they do not stand to block the blows I throw in your direction.

More bad dreams about box cutters and knives and things that will slice away at your puny little shell of a life? Speak for yourself Colin. You can't speak through others if their mouth does not move. You are a bad ventriloquist. Not a career for you. You have a career and that's running from yourself. Keep running Colin. I'm getting closer!

No One stands in your defense stalker. They all let me hunt you down.

239

And the next day, to all Colin's known emails, most of which were hijacked identities of my friends and colleagues, he sent the following ominous message:

"I'm coming to get you stalker!"[181]

The Hunter was stalking the Stalker, now prey.

Bear Scare

Colin wouldn't scare so easily, continuing threats to "pour hot oil" on Dustin's face, to put him in a wheelchair, to harm his family.[182] He blamed Dustin for "breaking up" our "relationship."

Dustin Bear-- you messed up my relationship with Leandra while she was on the ship by speaking evil on me.
Never mind in church I have prayed that Satan will ravage your family to the very core already
May your father and mother die slowly of cancer in front of your eyes soon and may you be run down by a car and die tragically.
never mess with someone else's girl.
you f**king loser-- you cheated your ex-girlfriend also a soprano singer of thousands of dollars before and now you want to mess up my relationship with Leandra

Colin M,
~~ "The "Cello Is Like A Beautiful Woman Who Has Not Grown Older, But Younger With Time, More Slender, More Supple, More Graceful." Pablo Casals ~~ [183]

While Colin was expending himself emotionally, Dustin was methodically sending him and his aliases thousands of emails, immobilizing existing email accounts in denial of service attacks.

The Hunter had done his homework... using Google Maps to locate exactly where Colin was, which restaurants he liked to frequent (Colin often sent pictures of himself to me from those restaurants—their metadata provided clues to his whereabouts), learning which Internet cafés he favored. He learned Colin's routines, the kinds of food he liked in the area, he found out about where he posed as a photographer. Then he published all that information on a blog he'd set up—www.cyberstalkers.org.

Dustin knew that he couldn't reach Colin through empathy; he suspected Colin was a sociopath. Causing him pain was the best solution, peaking with Dustin's email to Colin's Singapore neighbors, exposing him as a stalker and pervert. Even Colin's church received a copy.

Dustin correctly sensed that Colin would respect Dustin's fearlessness and consistent counterattacks. I don't think Colin knew what had hit him. I do know that for the first time in six years, Colin was afraid and pleaded with Dustin to stop.

The end result was slightly miscalculated, with Colin ceasing attacks on Dustin, but continuing to stalk me and my family.

Sex-calation

As the war between the Hunter and the Stalker waged, Colin continued to threaten and sexually abuse me—even more. The sex emails from Colin disgusted and embarrassed me. I felt ashamed. Rationalizing alone couldn't stanch those feelings.

Later that day, he writes:

"I wanted sex with you the whole day—I feel better now that I am much happier—Really---I felt I could soak your clothes in my ejaculations. It's getting uncontrollable. I think about you all the time—and looking at the photo of you in the red dress today did nothing to help the situation—I needed sex even more with you. I need you Leandra. I need to be very very very deep in you." [184]

I had plenty of these deviant communications from Colin, a self-proclaimed virgin, who explained his celibacy more than once.

"Sex to me is special and only in a marriage. I nearly felt God saying to me he would strike me there and then. I was afraid. It was also because I love God and you."[185]

His chastity and church talk (a self-proclaimed Christian, spouting the Bible, Colin often mentioned his church attendance) didn't stop him from writing smut.

I am driven into a sexual frenzy thinking about you Leandra-- I think we need to meet in NYC-- or never mind-- I will turn up at your house.
I have the condoms which I got from getting FHM Deutschland magazine... [186]

These emails still make me feel physically ill—there were thousands of them, sometimes several in one day.

I want to cum in you. I need to have children by you. I want to cum all over your face and hair and right into your sexy green eyes. I am a wildman now. Colin M. [187]

Several hours later, he wrote:

"I am getting you a pair of nude colored and another pair of black colored thigh highs Leandra...!" [188]

A cyber-rapist, Colin confused sex, love, violence, and power. He was as awkward sexually as he was violent in his threats to mutilate, disfigure and kill me. He was inexperienced sexually, asking me about whether he was right to abstain from sex when he entered and left college in the U.S., referring to his virginity in emails where he posed as Fritz Tan.

The sex emails from Colin were viscerally disgusting to me, causing me shame, fear, and embarrassment. Colin was now not only a stalker but also a pervert. They increased as my Internet contact with him decreased.

"....everyday I think about sex with you. I can no longer control myself anymore. I need to f**k and procreate. And I know how to get what I do want from you.
Colin M. [189]

"....I feel both sexy and sexual. I want to make love to you over and over again before you go on stage to sing on Friday...." [190]

"...my sexual desires are only for you. I need to be f**ked and f**ked by you Leandra." [191]

244

Violence Uptick

The violence, too, was extreme—it amazed me that I was still so scared by his words, but I could easily envision the rage, simply from his syntax, typographical errors, and typeface. The more uncontrolled they were, the more I had to fear. Sometimes he didn't bother writing anything other than a huge, rambling, violent boldfaced threat:

If I get really really angry—a lot of people are going to get injured, beaten and harmed Leandra---I have the ability to do it!!! All because of your actions and Dustin Bear's actions—set things right—its time to talk to me. [192]

Followed ten minutes later by:

I don't want to turn against you Leandra—but its your RESPONSIBILITY and DUTY to me to reconcile. Because if I turn into a monster—everything and everybody will be slashed into bits beginning with that balless creature DUSTIN BEAR. [193]

With a final threat to my sister, Courtney, one minute later:

You too Courtney—you bloody get f**king Dustin Bear as a friend off you facebook list! [194]

And then came the inevitable confluence of sex and violence, He was desperate and escalating:

I want to make love to you over and over and over again Leandra
I cannot take this stress and frustration anymore! [195]

In an August 5, 2010, email to my family (copied to Gale Martin of www.Operatoonity.com), Colin explains his increasing aggression as directly linked to his sexual frustration.

"I know I am being aggressive and playing a hard hand—because I am. Because my testosterone levels are rising with each day with all this work stress and pressure and I desire Leandra." [196]

More than ever, Colin was a ticking time bomb.

PART ELEVEN
LAW ENFORCEMENT ODYSSEY
PART DEUX

Singapore Police: Take Two

"Beginning in the spring of 2010, I tried to fight back again by going to the authorities. I filed a second police report with the Singapore Police Force."[197]

I received a confirming email from Singapore's Electronic Police Center on April 9, 2010, the same day, with a new report number, F/20100409/2147.[198]

On April 10, 2010, I followed up with a fax and an email:

"My name is Leandra Ramm. I am a US citizen. I am an actress and singer and have had a fair share of publicity on international Television. Over the past 4 years, a Singapore citizen has been stalking me. His name is "Colin Mak Yew Loong" and he has a criminal record. I have thousands of emails to prove this threatening ways and illegal activity. I can forward you some of those emails or anything you need. I sent him a "cease and desist" letter but he keeps stalking me and sending threats to me, my employers, family and friends. Is there anything you can do to help me?

The police, polite as always, retained their stance. "They would not be investigating my case further,"[199] writing:

"From the facts in your email we note that you received the emails while you were in US. As this is outside Singapore, it is outside Singapore Police jurisdiction to investigate. You are advised to lodge a report in your country and Singapore Police will render the necessary assistance if there is a request." [200]

Embassy Roadblocks

Sounding like a broken record, I sought help from two embassies: the American Embassy in Singapore and the Singapore Embassy in Washington, D.C.

To whom it may concern,

My name is Leandra Ramm. I am a US citizen and I am being stalked by a Singapore citizen. I have never met this man. The stalker's name is: Colin Mak Yew Loong. He is a known international criminal that has been in jail for his crimes. Colin Mak Yew Loong saw me on international television in 2006 and has been stalking me ever since. He is stalking me through email, Internet, phone and postal mail. Colin Mak Yew Loong is threatening my family, friends, my colleagues, employers and myself. He is harming my career, emotional well being and I am scared for my safety. I have been advised by my USA lawyer to contact you. Do you think you can help me with this case? I have spoken to the Singapore Police Force and they said they can not help me because there is no law that protects me from international cyberstalking and because of international borders. I have over a thousand emails from him, postal mail and voice mail recordings. Also, friends, family members and employers of mine are willing to testify as well. If you need any of this information from me, please let me know and I will send it over to you. I look forward to hearing from you. [201]

The American Embassy, Singapore American Citizen Services responded:

"Dear Ms. Ramm:
We regret you are experiencing the ordeal you have mentioned below. First, we are unclear as to where you are residing. If you live in Singapore, you may want to consider retaining a lawyer here....If you have filed a police report with the Singapore Police, it might be helpful to have record of it in our office. You may send it to us if you have. Again, we regret that you have had to endure this stalking. We cannot provide law enforcement for you, nor can we provide legal counsel.

If you are living in the U.S., you might want to contact the FBI if he is stalking you online. If you haven't already you might want to consider making a police report where you are already residing. Leaving a paper trail, documenting events, all may be helpful should things escalate.

Please consider what you can do to feel safe. It may cost time, money, but it might help your peace of mind in the long run." [202]

From the Singapore Embassy in D.C., I received this reply, whose tone was more in keeping with the Singapore Tourism Board than an embassy:

Dear Leandra,

Greetings from the Singapore Embassy in Washington DC. As much as we would like to be of help, there is not much that we can do from our end. While we empathise with you and do appreciate that this could be a case of a criminal nature (perhaps an aspect of harassment), it is best handled by the law enforcement authorities. We hope that you will appreciate that we not legally competent to offer you any advise on anti-stalking legislation in Singapore, and if there was such legislation, of its applicability to your particular case of cyberstalking across international borders. Your lawyer would be the best person to advise you in this respect. We note that you have already been in touch with the Singapore Police Force, and that they appear to be constrained in dealing with it. Under the circumstances, we regret that we are in no position to assist you in this matter. We hope that you understand our position. [203]

Best Regards.
MEJAR SINGH GILL
Counsellor (Admin & Consular)
Singapore Embassy in Washington DC
Singapore P.I.

I exhausted my resources with law enforcement and now, with diplomatic channels. I had tried every possible organization, embassy, political contact, even the U.N.-- and every single one had refused me.

I had lost confidence in the system; with flagging optimism I decided to take my fight to the private sector.

Singapore P.I.

In late 2010, I tried a "when in Rome" approach with Singapore—I hired a local firm to investigate Mak and to file a police report on my behalf. I knew about this private investigation office because a colleague of mine, Eryn Pola, had hired them to help her. She was one of my many friends and colleagues who Colin stalked because of her association with me. Her husband told me they used this P.I in 2007, and it seemed like a good idea to hire them again. I was hopeful that this P.I. office could be effective where I had failed—convincing the police to arrest Colin.

I received back a dossier confirming my stalker's name (Mak Yew Loong), a few aliases (Colin M, Colin T M, Colin, Miggy Miggy, and Stormo Rochalie), Singaporean citizenship and age (33), while revealing a transient predator recidivist, whose emails they traced to Singapore Internet locations. This dossier was updated after the 2007 report obtained by Pola.

The dossier validated what the Singapore and U.S. officials had refused to recognize—that Colin was a repeat offender cybercriminal on the loose and continuing to terrorize a growing international victim pool.

On November 3, 2010, the investigators wrote the Singapore police a detailed email, which included, as an attachment, the Harvard University police flyer warning about Colin's criminal trespassing years before.

"One of the cases that we are working on involves a stalker who has been sending threatening emails to cause grievous bodily harm to our client, an American. These threats are all made via email, though he has stalked her in the USA. We have traced him to a Singapore citizen Colin Mak. We believe that this man could be the same Colin Mak who has been convicted in Singapore in the past....Are you able to clarify what we can do to assist our client to arrest this Colin Mak. He may need to be in a mental facility. From the USA, we are seeking FBI support. However, they will need co-operation from our Singapore Police and hence we are facilitating the process on behalf of our client. We have evidence of all the threatening emails if required.... [204]

After filing the 2010 Singapore police report, I continued to receive Colin's death threats, several on December 22, 2010, which I forwarded to the investigators. [205]

you will be stalked and caught until I get an apology from you and all monies are returned.
you earned an estimated 20 000 USD while on board the ship---

Leandra--- Xmas is near-- if I get Abba my father to deal with you-- it is really the end of your career.
my .40 caliber P226 pistol is cocked and loaded. Don't make me unholster it.
-- Colin M,

~~ "The "Cello Is Like A Beautiful Woman Who Has Not Grown Older, But Younger With Time, More Slender, More Supple, More Graceful." Pablo Casals ~~

And, from Stormo Rochalie, Colin's alter ego:

"...if we are not reconciled (by December 28, 2010) I will send someone to slash that c**t face of yours in NYC." [206]

Singapore Sling Refrain

On Christmas Eve 2010, the investigative firm filed a new police report on my behalf with Singapore Police. Surely, now authorities had ample evidence to arrest Colin!

Singapore responded unequivocally on January 6, 2011:

"We have carefully looked into the police report number F/20100409/214 lodged by Ms Leandra Ramm and the information provided in your email. The case is classified as Intentional Harassment under Section 13A(1)(a) of the Miscellaneous Offences Act, Chapter 184 which is a non-arrestable offence...Please be informed that Police will also not be conducting further investigations into the matter..." [207]

Despite his death threats, Mak was, at most, guilty of "intentional harassment," pursuable in Singapore civil courts, but with no criminal implications.

I'd been slung again.

PART TWELVE
GALVANIZING THE PRESS

Court of Public Opinion

I had liberated myself from Colin in spring 2010. I was determined to fight back, despite the impotence of the criminal justice system and the apathy of embassies. Every time I would hear the word "No," or "We can't help you," I fought harder, tried different approaches. If the legal system would not stop my stalker, I would fight my case in the court of public opinion—the press.

It was time to complete the circle. Colin had learned about me through the media; now I would use the press to expose him!

Hiccups—Backstage Magazine

In December 2010, New York's *Backstage Magazine* published an article about stalking in the entertainment world, titled "Photo Copying." I was featured prominently and was generally elated that this story was out. I was no longer the pariah opera singer with the crazy stalker, who should have known better. The article provided me with validation I sorely needed, considering the onslaught of doubt I faced daily.

On December 16, 2010, I contacted the writer, Simi Horowitz:

From: Leandra Ramm <leandraramm>
Sent: Thursday, December 16, 2010 7:00 PM
To: Simi Horwitz
Subject: Thank you and great article!

Hi Simi, I saw the article in Backstage today! What a great article, very helpful and informative! Thank you very much for including my story and headshot. The "courses of action" section was especially helpful to me. Did you want to do a separate follow-up story on my situation as well?
Best, Leandra

Simi responded several days later:

Hi Leandra,
Thanks for your lovely note. Also, I want to thank you for your time and courtesy.
We are talking about a follow up. I'll keep you posted.
In the meantime, Happy Holidays.
Cheers,
Simi [208]

On January 20th, a month after Simi expressed interest in doing a follow up, I emailed her again.

From: Leandra Ramm <leandraramm>
Sent: Thursday, January 20, 2011 11:34 AM
To: Simi Horwitz
Subject: Re: Thank you and great article!

Hi Simi, Hope all is well! I just wanted to get back in touch and see if you were interested in doing a follow-up story. Thank you so much and all the best!
Leandra

Simi responded quickly:

It's still a possibility. But at this point, I'm bogged down with other projects. Are you still hearing from the stalker? Or has he disappeared? [209]

From: Leandra Ramm <leandraramm>
Sent: Thursday, January 20, 2011 1:36 PM
To: Simi Horwitz
Subject: Re: Thank you and great article!

Hi Simi, Thank you so much for your response, I'm sure you're very busy and I can't thank you enough for the time you put into the first article. Yes, I'm still hearing from the stalker unfortunately on a daily basis. I'm trying my best to ignore it as much as possible though and live my life and pursue my career as if he doesn't exist. I found that the article you wrote gave me a lot of strength in knowing that I have the business on my side and that I am stronger than him, even though the law can't do anything yet. Everyone I send the article to loves it and a more in-depth follow-up story would also be fantastic!
Best, Leandra

On Thu, Jan 20, 2011 at 1:44 PM, Simi Horwitz <shorwitz> wrote:

Hi Leandra.

Thanks for your continued kind words.
Just curious to know if the stalker commented on the article.

For whatever it's worth, he did contact Back Stage with all kinds of demented, incoherent threats. These were a series of ongoing emails, which we were told by the Back Stage lawyers to ignore.

Pursuing this story further is on a back burner mostly because of other more immediate projects. That said, I'm not sure the editors are going to think it's prudent to pursue this further because of the stalker's response. These are fearful times.
Simi

From: Leandra Ramm <leandraramm>
Sent: Thursday, January 20, 2011 2:12 PM
To: Simi Horwitz

Subject: Re: Thank you and great article!

That's a perfect example of what I constantly deal with: him contacting anything or anybody I am associated with and trying to create fear in their minds with empty threats to hurt my career and reputation. I have received emails from him about the article denying its truth and with a bunch of threats. I have not opened any of his emails recently, however, because I feel it is just hurting myself to read them. They are all pretty much the same: threats, twisted love letters, hate letters, etc. Of course it's the editor's choice if they want to print a follow-up story, but it's exactly what the article is about: increasing awareness about this cyberstalking phenomenon so that people can become more knowledgeable about internet stalkers and to not let them control our lives.
Leandra

On Thu, Jan 20, 2011 at 2:13 PM, Simi Horwitz <shorwitz> wrote:
Okay. The editor is now in Sundance. When he returns I'll bring it up again.

From: Leandra Ramm <leandraramm>
Sent: Thursday, January 20, 2011 2:20 PM
To: Simi Horwitz
Subject: Re: Thank you and great article!
Ok, thank you!
Leandra

On Thu, Jan 20, 2011 at 2:22 PM,
Simi Horwitz <shorwitz> wrote:
Have you ever met this man? Do you know his name?

From: Leandra Ramm <leandraramm>
Sent: Thursday, January 20, 2011 3:07 PM
To: Simi Horwitz <shorwitz>
Subject: Re: Thank you and great article!

I have never met him. His name is Colin Mak Yew Loong.

On Thu, Jan 20, 2011 at 3:08 PM,
Simi Horwitz <shorwitz> wrote:

Thanks.

I hadn't heard back from Simi, so I wrote her on February 14, 2011:

From: Leandra Ramm <leandraramm>

Sent: Monday, February 14, 2011 2:40 PM
To: Simi Horwitz <shorwitz>
Subject: Re: Thank you and great article!
Hi Simi, Hope all is well. Just wanted to quickly get back in touch to see if there was any interest in a follow-up story at this point. Thank you!
Leandra

On Mon, Feb 14, 2011 at 3:18 PM,
Simi Horwitz <shorwitz> wrote:

Hi Leandra,
We're still talking about it, but no commitment has been made.
I'll let you know.
Thanks for getting back to me.
Simi

On March 16, 2011, intending to download the "Photo Copying" article from *Backstage's* website, I discovered the article's link missing. I immediately contacted Simi.

From: Leandra Ramm <leandraramm>
Sent: Wednesday, March 16, 2011 12:39 PM
To: Simi Horwitz <shorwitz>
Subject: Re: Thank you and great article!

Hi Simi, Hope all is well. I just quickly wanted to ask if you had the link to the first article I was in 'Photo Copying'. I searched for it on backstage and it's no longer there as well as I did a search on the Backstage website. Thanks so much!
Leandra

On Wed, Mar 16, 2011 at 12:48 PM,
Simi Horwitz <shorwitz> wrote:

Hi Leandra,
Regrettably, it was removed because your friend threatened to have me "beaten up and raped" unless the article was pulled. Yes, his intimidating tactics won. I'm sorry.
Simi

I was shocked at her categorization of Colin as my "friend." What an outrage! I had been wrong about the *Backstage* progressive mindset. Again, the "blame the victim" mentality prevailed. It was sickening.

From: Leandra Ramm <leandraramm>
March 16, 2011 1:00 PM
To: Simi Horwitz <shorwitz>
Subject: Re: Thank you and great article!

Gosh, I'm very sorry to hear that. The cyberstalker whom I never met, NOT my friend, can never get in the country just so you know. The FBI, Singapore police, NYPD, my private investigator and my personal lawyer and all authorities have told me he is stuck in Singapore and will never be allowed in the USA, there is a red flag on his passport. If that is any consolation. They have also told me repeatedly that there is nothing they can do to help me because they are just emails and he is not breaking any laws in Singapore and there are no laws yet for International cyber stalking. I hope I can still have a career and people can look past this as it has had quite a negative effect on my career thus far as I'm sure you can imagine.
Leandra

On Wed, Mar 16, 2011 at 1:07 PM
Simi Horwitz <shorwitz> wrote:

Of course, he's not your friend, anything but. I should have put "friend" in quotes. I filed a complaint with the police, but they said there was nothing they could do. They simply don't have the man power.

From: Leandra Ramm leandraramm
Sent: Wednesday, March 16, 2011 1:13 PM
To: Simi Horwitz shorwitz
Subject: Re: Thank you and great article!

Yep, there is nothing that any of the authorities can do unfortunately. That is why I wanted to get this story out in the public, to make people aware of this problem. It is quite amazing that nothing can be done when somebody so clearly is breaking laws...even though there are no "laws". It is quite astonishing that in 2011 people can get away with this. I'm sorry Backstage felt they had to pull the article. I thought it was an important article and the story needed to be told.
Leandra

From: Simi Horwitz <shorwitz>
Date: March 16, 2011 1:19:04 PM EDT
To: Leandra Ramm <leandraramm>
Subject: RE: Thank you and great article!

They pulled it because there are just too many liability issues here. In the highly unlikely event something happened to me, bla, bla, bla...

For whatever it's worth, the detective I spoke with said cyber issues will be the next big area in need of guidelines and policing.

Was she kidding me? What kind of reporting was this? The "next big area" in cyber issues was here and now! I was living it.

Apparently, the days of inveterate reporting were long gone, superseded by the more pressing "liability issues" and the bottom line.

London Telegraph Gaffe

Hoping that my *Backstage* experience in New York was a fluke, I granted an interview with London's *Sunday Telegraph* a few months later. The subject was not cyberstalking, but the Repository for Germinal Choice. Always supportive, David Plotz had recommended the writer speak with me and my sister Courtney.

From: Lucinda Everett <lucinda.everett>
Date: Thu, 17 Mar 2011 14:30:34 +0000
To: Leandra Ramm <leandraramm>
Subject: Interview request with the Sunday Telegraph

Hi Leandra,
I hope you are well and having a good week so far.
I write for The Sunday Telegraph in the UK and wondered if you might be available for a very quick chat today or tomorrow morning? I am writing a short piece about the children who were born as a result of the Repository for Germinal Choice and what they are up to these days. I have already spoken to David Plotz who passed me your details and suggested you get in touch.
It would be great if you could get back to me as soon as possible to let me know if you are available for a chat.
All the best,
Lucinda

I responded eagerly to the opportunity.

Hi Lucinda,

Thank you for the email! Yes I'm available tomorrow morning and would be interested in doing an interview with you.

I have to let you know, however, that I have a cyberstalker that violently attacks any article I am in that comes out online. If the article comes out online and your email address is public or the Sunday Telegraph email addresses are publicly online he will most likely start flooding your email with violent threats. This man saw me on a CNN show I did in 2006 about the repository and hasn't stopped cyber stalking me since. A recent interview I did (ironically about cyber stalking) was removed because the newspaper was so scared of the threats. My private investigator, lawyer, FBI and New York Police all have confirmed that this man lives in Singapore and can not get out of his country, they are just emails and should be ignored.

My lawyer has advised me to tell people in advance of this problem.

If you would still like to do the interview I would love to. Please let me know what you would like to do.

Thank you,
Leandra [210]

I guess honesty was not the best policy; it would actually be my unraveling. As with the *Backstage* incident, the lawyers would thwart me again!

From: Lucinda Everett <lucinda.everett>
Date: Fri, 18 Mar 2011 12:28:02 +0000
To: Leandra Ramm <leandraramm>
Subject: Re: Interview request with the Sunday Telegraph

Hi Leandra,
Apologies for not coming back to you - yesterday got really really busy!

On speaking to my editor, we've actually decided to write the piece without mentioning you by name. David Plotz mentioned you and your sister in one of his quotes so I have kept that in but have just called you a 'pair of sisters'. David has described you as appealing, fun and talented!

I do hope that the piece doesn't spark any more horrible emails to you and thanks again for the offer of help.
All the best,
Lucinda

On 18 March 2011 12:55, <leandraramm>□
wrote:□□
□□
□□□□□□□□□□□□□□□□□□□□□□□□□□

Hi Lucinda,

Thank you for getting back to me. Just to be clear, I would love to do the interview. I was just being up front about my cyberstalker situation as my lawyer has advised me to do so. I was informing you for the newspaper's sake, not my own. I'm trying to be in the spotlight actually, not back away from it. I am personally not worried about the cyberstalker emails, they go directly to my trash. My lawyer is helping take care of any repercussions the cyberstalker has.

On a side note, I will be coming to the UK this Spring to do a promotional tour so having my name mentioned would actually help me when coming over there. I would really like to do the interview and am available today. I'm sorry if my first email gave the wrong impression.

Thank you!
Leandra

And the final blow:

From: Lucinda Everett <lucinda.everett>
Date: Fri, 18 Mar 2011 14:16:43 +0000
To: leandraramm
Subject: Re: Interview request with the Sunday Telegraph

Hi Leandra,

I'm so sorry but we won't be able to include your name. The editor was worried about you but is also concerned about me and my name being attached to the piece, so he would prefer to run without your name.

Thank you so much for being upfront with us and I'm sorry that your honesty has made you miss out on a piece of publicity but we really appreciate you letting us know.

All the best,
Lucinda

I'd experienced the same faint-heartedness with traditional press on both sides of the pond. Maybe I'd have a better chance with social media.

Operatoonity Knocks

I gave an interview to *Operatoonity*, an online Opera blog, whose editor Gale Martin, "tweeted" the request. I happily obliged. The interview, a small biopic of my life as a young opera performer, came out one day before I ended my "at bay" accord with Colin, never to speak, text or email him again.

About three hours before I ended all communications, I received an email from Miggy Miggy, who explained:

"I am writing to you in the midst of a lot of hurt, anger and pain after discovering you spent time with a Twitter citizen instead o me. I am totally prepared to strike pre-emptively this time round. This shows I was not on your mind." [211]

Mak, as usual, feeling slighted, although the actual interview occurred five months previous to its publication, was determined to terrorize Gale into removing the article from her blog. Posing as Stormo Rochalie, he writes to Gale, copying my parents and me:

Gale martin
I have a nice favor to ask of you.
I would like you to take down, yes DELETE the entire interview you did with Leandra Ramm till I can resolve my ongoing crisis with her...Gale—if you do not take down the webpage—I shall have to pay a personal visit to her mother at the ballet school in which Adrienne Ramm plays the piano. Things can get unpleasant—I am very deeply hurt and can be irrational...I am a passionate person who demands loyalty and honesty.
People will be physically hurt with weapons... [212]

And two minutes later:

Gale Martin
--you delete this interview here—till I start talking with Leandra again or else people are going to get beaten up, hurt permanently, etc. ..I can even meet you in person for a nice talk about why you are aiding the enemy. [213]

Gale didn't remove the content, despite Colin's threats. I told her to ignore his emails, but they kept coming. When I later asked her to feature me for something else having to do with my singing, she said "No" ... not an unexpected response, considering.

I still commend her for not removing my interview, which remains posted on the Operatoonity blog.

The United Kingdom Network for Surviving Stalking

The Economist would rehabilitate my flagging respect for journalists, editors, and the media in general. I would come to the attention of that respected publication through a circuitous route, beginning with Becky Marks of Scarlett Entertainment, my London management company.

By virtue of representing me, Becky was one of Colin's "collateral damage" victims, receiving many threats directed at me and at her, her associates and the company. Other companies would have dropped me, but Becky was sympathetic and actually connected me to someone who really helped me, Alexis Bowater, CEO of the Network for Surviving Stalking, a/k/a the NSS.

Bowater, a well-respected news personality, hailed from the English aristocracy and was herself a cyberstalker survivor. She had legal expertise, a reputable and effective organization and, most crucial, a sterling personal reputation. Aligning myself with Alexis and NSS gave me much-needed validation. In stark contrast to law enforcement advice, Alexis encouraged me to fight back. I was a stalker "survivor," not just a "victim."

In an email of March 13, 2011, she wrote:[214]

"Leandra, please persevere with this. I know that it is hard but the best thing you can do in this situation is to keep fighting if you can and feel strong enough. I have tried to get as many important and influential people on board as I can and we are all behind you, but international cyberstalking is an area that really needs to be addressed and unfortunately you are at the forefront of the changes we are determined to make."

Alexis then offered me what would become a pivotal opportunity. The timing was providential.

"If you wanted I could put you in touch with a journalist who is writing an article for The Economist magazine, she is doing an article on cyberstalking and would be very interested in talking to you."

As the English say, it was "sorted." I took Alexis up on the offer.

Restoring My Faith—The Economist

I received an email from an *Economist* journalist, friends with Alexis. I warned the journalist that Colin would terrorize her for writing about me. *The Economist*[215] protected the author's identity and I won't breach that trust here, although I do see a certain irony in the source (me) protecting the press.[216]

From: XXXX <[Economist columnist]>
Date: Wed, 30 Mar 2011 17:05:41 +0100
To: leandraramm
Cc: <XXXX>
Subject: Economist newspaper article on cyber-stalking

Dear Leandra,

Alexis from NSS in the UK kindly gave me your contact details (after checking with you first). As I think Alexis explained, I'm writing a piece for the Economist's international section on the difficulty of policing and prosecuting cyber-stalking cases, particularly across jurisdictions, as I know you have been unlucky enough to find out. If you're happy for me to send you a couple of questions that would be great.

>> I know that you made Alexis aware that anyone who wrote about you would also be targeted. I have taken advice from the editor of the International section and they will not even put my name on the pay-roll for this article, so as long as everyone I talk to keeps it confidential who is writing it, hope that your stalker won't be able to target me or anyone else from the Economist. As I was also cyber-stalked myself I'm well aware of how awful your predicament is and I can only extend my sympathy to you and hope that by writing this piece it highlights the issues raised by your case. I am not going to identify myself as the author of this anywhere, anyway, as I don't want my stalker rearing his ugly head again anyway!

On Wed, Mar 30, 2011 at 10:57 PM, <leandraramm> wrote:

Hi XXXX,
Thank you for the email. Great, I would love to answer some questions and get this story out there to the public! I think everyone should become aware of cyberstalking. Thanks so much! Looking forward to your questions.
Leandra

The Economist published my story, "Creepy crawlies....the Internet allows the malicious to menace their victims" in its April 20, 2011, print edition.

My guess is that Singapore's top officials, avid readers of *The Economist*, a publication the Prime Minister, who coincidentally shared a surname with my stalker, had successfully sued for criticizing its regime, checked the veracity of the contents. And finding them accurate, they began to feel the pressure of the international media.

This single article, coupled with one well-placed, surreptitious phone call from a man named A.J. Fardella to a Secret Service acquaintance with connections in Singapore, would tip the scales against Colin. Finally.

PART THIRTEEN
REDEEMED

The Italian Job

In 2008, Walnut Creek, California, I met Jimmy Coniglio, a professional biologist whose hobby was singing and acting. We were both performing in Diablo Valley Light Opera's *Man of La Mancha*. This was my first crossover performance from opera and more into a musical theater repertoire. Colin's constant stalking and harassment had poisoned the opera world against me and I against it. I was ready for a change and hopeful that Colin would leave me alone once I had left the art form he loved best.

Later, Jim would comment on the irony of performing *La Mancha*, considering its subject matter—the Inquisition. We began a romantic relationship, at which time he saw the effects of Colin's inquisition-like tactics on me. Many times, I had to "go make a call" to Colin; I had begun my accord with Colin, a/k/a the "at bay" period, which meant that although the threats had abated somewhat, they were always lurking if I failed to contact Colin as scheduled. I was a slave to Colin's scheduled phone conversations, and later on, to his chats.

Jimmy was upset for me, but didn't have any ideas about how to handle Colin. Unlike the other two boyfriends, he never got directly involved with Colin. He never contacted Colin, and Colin never knew he existed.

At the time, I still had faith in my "at bay" arrangement and defended it—insisting that everything was under control as long as I kept my end of the bargain. The following year, I came back to that area of California, working for the Willows Theater, and stayed with Jim. We were still in a romantic relationship—that was why I performed with another theatre in his area. We didn't break up until after I went back to New York, although we remained good friends.

That summer, he saw firsthand more of Colin's stalking, even though Colin and I were still "at bay," meaning Colin was violating the terms of our agreement and I was letting him get away with it. Jimmy was concerned for me—I was exhibiting signs of stress and was jumpy and filled with anxiety. Just on a human level, no matter what, he said, no one deserved this. He really wanted to help me.

Several months later, he did, by connecting me with A.J. Fardella.

Fardella, like Coniglio, was from Pittsburg, California, a tight-knit community with a large Italian-American population. I had originally met A.J. at Pittsburg's Italian-American Club in the summer of 2008, where James and I performed an operatic duet in Italian for a number of prominent Italo-Americans, including the newly elected head of the Sons of Italy . They all had a soft spot for opera.

We brought the house down.

The Tipping Point

In February 2010, Jimmy and A.J. Fardella worked together on a data forensics security project for a mutual client—another notable, powerful Italian family in the area. A.J. and Jimmy became close. Their work required a strict code of silence and discretion, and they developed a mutual respect and business friendship.

In spring of 2010, shortly after their project completion, Jim was driving from Pittsburg to Modesto—about 72 miles, when divine intervention struck—that's how he described it. A.J. was the man who could help me with this Colin mess. Jim called me as soon as he reached Modesto— he knew this guy; we'd actually met in Pittsburg at the Italian Club back in 2009. I was willing to learn more, so I told him it was okay to discuss but I was not very hopeful,.

Jimmy called A.J. to set up a meeting. As was their practice, they kept phone conversations *de minimis*— there's a thing with this guy—let's meet. Soprano-speak.

The meeting took place somewhere in the vicinity of A.J.'s cyber forensics offices, unobtrusively. Jimmy explained my situation with Colin, its origins with the genius sperm bank media blitz, its international reach and long duration, the voluminous mass of data—a multi-media assault of unparalleled magnitude.

The case fascinated him, but he had to think about it. His data forensics business, Black Diamond Data was a small shop, just he and his wife. A.J. knew he was the best man to handle the case because of his unique collection of resources.

He was apprehensive, but the case excited him—it was all-consuming. He knew that while it would be the case of a lifetime, it would undoubtedly exhaust his attention and most of his resources—and there were no guarantees that he'd be successful. On the fence, he called Jimmy and asked him one question, which would determine my fate:

"Do you still love and care about this girl?" He said that he did.

Now, before even speaking with me, A.J. would face his biggest hurdle—convincing the company lawyer, his wife.

Dance of Trust

A few days later, I called A.J. in a "dance of trust" phone call. I had been pushed and pulled, disappointed and elated so many times at this point, most egregiously by people with "expertise" in cybercrimes, who amounted to no more than ineffectual email pushers. I was too emotionally tired to go through another soar-and-crash.

One thing was certain. A.J. wanted to be paid for this project. He wasn't offering his services for free. What's more, he steadfastly refused to guaranty any result. He cautioned me to avoid those who promised results—they were opportunistic charlatans. Success was unlikely, as I'd already learned. He wasn't going to get my hopes up. I appreciated his candor.

The final agreement between us contained some hard-won provisions, including a regular payment schedule and specific actions he and Black Diamond Data would take on my behalf.

Ultimately, what got Colin arrested had more to do with the Singaporean concept of "face" and the human element brought by A.J. than the evidence alone.

48-Hour Man

On April 11, 2011, Fardella drove 363 miles from Norfolk, Virginia, where he'd attended a family wedding ceremony over the weekend, nonstop to New York City. He went directly to our historical Brooklyn flat, where Dustin and I met him for the first time.

A.J. arrived about 9:30 at night after driving all day. Despite the long journey, A.J. looked sharp in a navy designer suit complete with a D.C. inside crowd must-have accessory—a U.S. Secret Service pin. We all shook hands. I ushered A.J. into the byzantine maze from the street-level building entry of the flat. I apologized for the appearance of my flat, a mess because I was moving out. My next gig was on another cruise ship, this time to the Caribbean.

Dustin was still fired up about the whole Colin ordeal, but quickly realized that I was in good hands with A.J. and was happy to pass the warrior baton to him. The three of us had a very high-amplitude discussion about the whole case, the culmination of which was our mutual decision that A.J.'s highest use was to do a forensic collection from both of our computers, starting immediately.

Dustin and A.J. worked well together, implementing a universally compliant data collection system, which collated all the different pieces of evidence from their various repositories.

Fardella insisted on gathering every email even remotely connected to the case, every voice mail, everything we had. This collection wasn't going to be representational—it would be exhaustive.

And exhausting. A.J. worked until 3 or 4 in the morning. He was delirious when he left. Later, he told me he had gone to walk in the park—at once depleted from the drive and ensuing work, but also elated. This case was going to be *huge!* It was a case that a data forensic examiner waits a lifetime for. It was a perfect match: I was in need of rescuing, and A.J. dreamt of a case as extreme as this to define his whole career.

Arresting Developments: The United States Secret Service

Retaining Black Diamond Data would prove to be the single best decision I would make in my fight against Mak. A.J. was certified, trained, and on the bleeding edge of cybercrime. He had been doing investigative work for years, and he had made many friends in federal law enforcement during his tenure as a teacher of various complex software programs. His students included Al, a Secret Service Agent, who would become one of his greatest friends. Through Al, A.J. learned and became a member of the San Francisco Electronic Crimes Task Force, run by the U.S. Secret Service, whose expertise was large scale cybercrime.

Armed with the evidence gathered during our blitzkrieg session in New York, A.J. placed a call to a contact in the U.S. Secret Service. The Service ran a cybercrimes training center in Singapore. It would take contact from an agent[217] who ran that facility to convince Singapore to take me seriously.

A.J.'s call began the momentum that would result in Colin's arrest. The Secret Service training center's head, David Chaney, contacted Singapore police, who sent me the following email on May 11, 2011:

Dear Madam,

1 refer to your emails to SPF Customer Relations Branch.

2 We wish to inform you that we are reviewing your Police report and the information provided by your lawyers. We have also received the documents sent to us. On completion of our investigations, we will consult the Attorney-General's Chambers with our findings. You will be informed of the outcome in due course.

3 If you have further information, please contact Chief Investigation Officer Gordon Toh at email address:
Gordon_Toh@spf.gov.sg or you may wish to call him at telephone number 6218-1215.

Yours faithfully,

STALKING A DIVA

DAVID CONCEICAO, ASP
INVESTIGATION DEVELOPMENT OFFICER
ANG MO KIO POLICE DIVISION

After "the phone call," supported by some of the more representative evidence, Singapore had no choice to but to arrest and incarcerate Colin, or lose face.

Singapore Police arrested Colin on July 24, 2011, just a couple of days before my 27th birthday. It was by far the best birthday present—ever.

A Little Help from My Friends

On July 26, 2011, I sent an email out to current and past employers, friends, and family members, even former boyfriends. I was ecstatic to hear that my tormentor was in jail. But there was a lot of work to be done to keep him there.

In order to secure Colin's conviction, Fardella and I worked tirelessly in producing an evidence package, complying with international evidence-handling standards, of the 5,000 emails, blogs, chat logs, and other communications. We needed all the help we could get, so I sent the following email to about 300 people:

Greetings,

You all know the nightmare I have been living through over the last 6 years because of the suspected stalker Collin Mak. There has been a break in the case and the Singapore Police Force has arrested him. Obviously I am overjoyed by this, but the story isn't over until he is convicted in a Singapore Court.

I have hired a Data Forensics Expert, A.J. Fardella to handle the thousands of pieces of evidence in this case and corroborate this evidence to support Mr. Mak's prosecution by the Singapore authorities.

Will you please take a small amount of your time and allow Mr. Fardella to contact you regarding the case? He promises to be brief and to the point.

I want to express my gratitude to everyone for his or her patience and support during this very trying time and ask you now to help put this menace in prison where he belongs and will no longer be a threat to, or threatening anyone.

Please let me know if Mr. Fardella may contact you regarding the case.

Thanks,
Leandra

As I expected, except for a few very close friends, the response was practically non-existent. People were frightened at Colin's repercussions for cooperating with Singapore authorities or even just talking to A.J. Frankly, if I put myself in the shoes of the recipients, especially those who were mere acquaintances or long-ago former co-workers, I don't know that I would have responded differently. Who wants to risk peace and career to help someone barely familiar, long ago?

There's a Latin expression, commonly used in the law, *res ipsa loquitur,* meaning, "the thing speaks for itself." I think it fits many aspects of this case, including the personalities of the two men who, respectively, triggered the beginning (MWL) and end (Dustin Bear) to Colin's stalking.

Quite predictably, Michael Wade Lee not only refused to assist, but emphatically told Fardella never to communicate with him again. Dustin Bear, on the other hand, offered to help the investigation in any way he could, even though he and I were no longer an item romantically. *Res ipsa loquitur.*

Blogspot Redemption

Things were going my way, even in the matter of Colin's defamatory blogs, where he had the unmitigated cheek to use my name and my images to post harmful lies about me. In May 2011, I had complained to Google that although I'd been successful in my Digital Millennium Copyright Act complaint against Mak, Google had failed to take down the offending blogs--divasgonewild and the musicdictator.com.

Although I credit my New York attorney, Monroe Mann, for getting me the successful outcome DMCA outcome, it was A.J. who used the buzz words that would convince Blogger to remove the repugnant material. I forwarded his September 13, 2011 email to the Blogger Team.

"I'm hoping you can assist me in the removal of certain blog content, both criminal and terrorist in nature, which targets Leandra Ramm...This content was posted by Colin Mak Yew Loong, who has just been arrested by the Singapore Police Force for CyberCrimes against Leandra Ramm. The blogs in question are listed below:

http://themusicdictator.blogspot.com
http://divasgonewild.blogspot.com

These blogs contain fabricated and fraudulent images and other content, which have been posted solely to harm Ms. Ramm, by destroying her professional and personal reputation, and most alarmingly, by threatening and terrorizing her and her associates into doing what Mr. Mak dictates. There are over 4,917 separate emails from the suspect to Leandra and her family and associates, some of which threaten to kill and inflict bodily harm on Ms. Ramm and/or, her family, friends and acquaintances. The blogs further bolster and support the threatening presence and tactics that the suspect has perpetrated on Ms. Ramm. We are finally making progress in Ms. Ramm's six year battle to retain her dignity and re-capture some peace from the punishment she has sustained at the hands of this cyber-terrorist. Ms. Ramm's goals include immediate removal of the blogs from public viewing.

Both of these blog locations have been archived for evidentiary purposes and will not impeded the current case being prosecuted if they are removed.

On behalf of Ms. Ram and myself, I want to thank you in advance for your guidance in removal of this material. Every day that this content is online is another day of suffering for the victim Leandra Ramm.[218]

Ten days later, Google took down the blogs.

Out and About!

This is what gets me about Singapore. They arrest Colin, then free him on his own recognizance, a failed recipe for a recidivist who can access a computer anywhere, create an identity and stalk without trace.

On November 11, 2011, A.J. called me with the bad news. Mohammedd Rafeek Kader, the Singapore investigator assigned to Colin's case had just informed him that the Singapore Police had released Colin.

I was floored. What about the arrest, what about a trial? I was willing to go to Singapore to put him behind bars, where he'd have no Internet access. Fardella told me that Colin was under a type of house arrest, where he would report to Singapore Police every Monday. There was no other oversight. Predictably, Colin was up to his old tricks in a matter of days.

On November 8, 2011, in performing a routine Google search, Fardella discovered that Colin had started up again, this time in a new blog.[219] The return address was spitzer50, a variation on one of Colin's monikers., A.J. again contacted Singapore police, this time with an evidence package, which included this new information and a threatening fax Colin had sent to my mother, Adrienne, at her employer, Ballet Academy East.

The fax was typical Colin cyber-terrorism:

"Get your daughter Leandra Ramm to talk to me and I will not carry out the beating and blinding of Bear, the saxophonist in due time...I pray the time will not come when I have to confront you at Ballet East, break things, etc to ask you to ask Leandra to repent."

It was important that Singapore had not only emails but hard evidence, like the fax, like the gifts he gave me— including lingerie with his DNA on it, and, much later, the letters he sent me in the mail. We would not give up this fight until Colin was stopped.

PART FOURTEEN
THE WAITING IS THE HARDEST PART

Mr. Fardella Goes to Washington

In the last week of March 2012, A.J. Fardella had two priorities when he flew into Washington Dulles International Airport. The first was his oldest son's wedding. The second was the International Chiefs of Police "Day on the Hill" in the Capitol. Spring-boarding from Day on the Hill was his meeting with Representative George Miller and Senator Diane Feinstein.

Fardella's objectives were simple—advocating implementation of the "three T's" with respect to cyber evidence and crimes: treaties, training, and tools.

A.J. launched into his presentation by handing out copies of Salonga's Contra Cost Times article, "Cyber Sleuth," to Congressional aides. Later, he summarized it for me:

> While our country has the legal infrastructure to handle cybercrime, we need international cooperation in the form of treaties. We need to lock up criminals who harm U.S. citizens, no matter where their physical body resides!
>
> The lack of treaties, combined with too little training and too few tools, generates a perfect storm for acquittal and a climate fostering even more internet crimes. As these offenses are not winnable, the United States Attorney rarely prosecutes electronic crimes. And yet the numbers of cybercrime, including cyber-stalking and harassment are increasing astronomically, according to FBI and Secret Services data.

Fardella finished by advocating a consistent, "templatized" training process for cyber crime handling and that law enforcement receive appropriate tools, only befitting for a state and country which birthed the Internet culture.

The reality was that most crimes committed have some "cyber" elements; lack of it, or lack of its proper handling, could lose a case.

Docudrama U.K. Style

I'd arrived in London on May 14th, 2013 to tape an hour-long segment for **Investigation *Discovery's*** true crime series launching in November, tentatively called "Obsessed" and focusing on stalking survivors. It was **I.D.**'s show, but ***October Films*** was producing, directing, and writing the series.

Producers at ***October Films*** learned of my story from the short-lived, "My Life is a **Lifetime** Movie," franchise, devoting a half-hour to my stalking nightmare. The ***Lifetime*** version, produced by ***Diga Productions***, played pretty fast and loose with the facts, like melding all my boyfriends over the past decade into Dustin. That bothered me, more in its implications about me, making me doubt myself. Did ***Lifetime*** consider three boyfriends over six years excessive for their mother-daughter demographic?

Diga-Lifetime's fudging the facts was one thing, but some of their tactics were downright unlawful—no wonder they wanted an air-tight release! Still, I balked when producers encouraged me to claim, on camera, that I'd had to take a cruise ship job just to pay my bill to A.J for his work on my case. That wasn't accurate; I was packing to go on the cruise even before A.J. collected the data in my Brooklyn flat. I objected to this mistaken rendition of the facts, at the same time realizing that I was not at liberty to divulge the terms of the contract, which was protected by a confidentiality agreement. ***Diga*** and ***Lifetime*** knew what they were demanding from me would harm my relationship with Fardella and would cast him in a disparaging false light.

Diga did not consider my relationship with Fardella their problem; they had contractual rights to the footage they filmed of me, end of story. I learned later, that apart from the rating spikes it was hoping to achieve, Diga had a more personal reason for making Fardella look unsavory on camera (including their changing his business title to

"International Businessman" from "data forensics expert" they'd previously agreed on. Some theorized that *Diga* was inflicting payback for A.J.'s refusal to sign the network's boilerplate, overreaching *Release from Liability*. (He called it "drinking the KoolAid.") *Diga's* workaround to Fardella's impertinence would be to portray him as a mysteriously shady "businessman," while insinuating problems in our two-year-old business relationship, up-'til-now a paragon of peacefulness and collaboration.

In contrast my *October Film's* experience in London was "what you see is what you get," balanced with an undercurrent of urgency to get the piece filmed on schedule. I attributed more "street cred" to *October Films,* in part because they seemed more interested in the substance of my story than how put together I appeared on camera! While *Diga's* professional makeup and hair people primped A.J. and me for the few minutes we appeared on camera, *October Films* was unapologetic in informing me the day before shooting began, and to my shock and horror, that hair and makeup was my responsibility. Maybe the rationale for a nonexistent beauty budget was that docudrama, was more documentary (no makeup) than feature film.

Luckily, I'd picked up a few hair and makeup tricks over the years in television and for opera and musical theater productions. I didn't know it yet, but I'd be requiring more than a little touchup for the tears I was about to shed on camera.

Alexis the Advocate

I arranged for Alexis Bowater, founder of Britain's Network for Surviving Stalking to meet me at the *October Films* studio in London's environs. Bowater, a former news anchorwoman was undeterred by the camera equipment and operators, producers and directors nor by me, the talent. Bowater was in her element—a newsworthy story— and the topic one she'd lectured on and supported internationally for years—helping survivors of stalking, like herself, cope.

Bowater's empathy, so apparent in her emails and calls with me, was evident on her face and in her mannerisms, too. It felt like having a mother on the set— to protect me from my stalker, if only by supporting my courage at continuing to fight against him. I felt I knew Alexis, but realized I hadn't even seen a recent photograph.

The doors to the Edwardian were open, so simultaneously knocked while greeting the film crew and producers in the downstairs kitchen area. Recognizing her immediately, less by her features, more by her strong and positive energy and good humor, I immediately stood up and embraced her holding her in a tight vintage American hug. Under the circumstances, even a reserved Englishwoman would have forgiven the Yank display of affection. Alexis, poised and kind, returned the hug, then cocking her head to one side, asked me how I'd been.

Our tea break was almost up, and our filming schedule tight, but I managed to introduce Bowater to our producer and to the interviewer, Jaime, who was about to ask me some of the toughest questions about Colin, retrieved from my book. My heart was beating a mile a minute.

Looking at Bowater for the first time, I wasn't surprised to see a perfect modern English lady, exhibiting classic, fine-boned features, framed by wheat colored hair casually revealing lovely skin, and a fit, lithe build.

Spot of Tea

As it turned out, Alexis had arrived at the October Film Studios during the emotionally toughest, and most embarrassing part for me—reading aloud Colin's sexual chat and emails, then processing them on camera.

Alexis was riveted, especially at one point which caused me to break down, when I was quoting Colin saying he'd like to c*m on my face. Jaime wanted me to read the line from that email. I began to read, then couldn't' stop myself from sobbing.

Later, Alexis remarked to me that Jaime, the interviewer "went a little too far in his questioning—that "it was a bit much," a typically understated and stoic British attitude, which, while protective of me, was also matter of fact and businesslike.

Bowater's stalker had fallen for her on the nightly news, becoming obsessed, during Bowater's second pregnancy. Most of her stalker's communication was through emails. But one day only a couple of weeks before the baby was due, she met her stalker in a scene straight out of Hitchcock. Bowater was home with alone with her older child, a toddler, when she sensed a presence behind her in the kitchen. She spun around, carefully enough to protect the baby she carried, to face her stalker. He said something completely mundane, while she prayed for the police.

Needless to say, it was quite serendipitous to have Alexis the Advocate watching my interview from the wings. I believed she'd handle my pain for me. Which she essentially did, when after the interview, she said something like, "shall I make some tea?" quipping that tea was the English way of dealing with crisis; a stiff upper lip and a cup of tea.

Oh, how I love the English!

Singapore Swing

Following his 2011 arrest, then release, Colin was still visiting the Singapore Police every Monday. The weekly check-ins were mandatory; a condition for Colin's release while the investigation was ongoing. For the most part, arresting Colin stopped his terrorism of me with a few final whimpers late in 2011.

Ironically, while under this quasi-house arrest, Mak had begun attacking Fardella in false blogs, accusing him of rape, warning his family of his penchant for young girls and using his well-known tactic of referencing some truths, like the picture of A.J. with Ice-T, in the midst of mostly lies .

I asked A.J. why he hadn't told the Singapore police to have Colin remove the content. He replied, "I consider it a badge of honor to be stalked by him. Until he is put away, I want that material to appear as a reminder that while he is out on the streets, anyone can become Colin's victim."

The Singaporean pendulum, in Colin's favor at the time of his 2011 release, began to swing our way when a fresh team of investigators and a female Deputy Public Prosecutor showed a renewed interest in trying Colin criminally.

The news from the grapevine was that this prosecutor was outraged and wanted Colin put away for life, if possible. She and her investigative team were searching through all the emails, and isolating the terrorist threats from mere harassment. They wanted as many counts as possible to slap on Mak.

Mohammed Amirudin, the newest investigator to have inherited my case, wrote Fardella on March 11, 2013,

"Good Day Mr Fardella,

The case have went out Attorneys and we are in the

process in deciding on the number of charges to proceed against Colin.

After a lengthy discussion at the attorneys office, there were a few

things that they want me to check with you before we can decided to

proceed on any court proceedings. We also found out that the affidavit

produced by you could not be used in court as it does not satisfy our

Legislation."[220]

Since my original affidavit, which had taken me weeks to assemble, didn't satisfy Singapore law, I'd have to start from scratch. Even then, there were no guarantees that Singapore would prosecute. I wondered whether this limbo would ever end.

Badge of Honor

Fardella called Colin's online attacks against him a badge of honor, which he eventually planned to use as proof that Mak was subverting the house arrest arrangement with the Singapore Police Force, just by logging on to the Internet, not to mention actively stalking while under their watch.

Fardella was waiting for an opportune moment to show his hand. It came in the form of an email from Eddie Tan, Mohamed Amirudin's boss and lead investigator on Singapore's case against Colin, who, on March 26, 2012, revealed some not-so-encouraging news,

> "We have recently seen the Deputy Public Prosecutor on Colin Mak's case and we were directed to gather further evidences before the case is good for further court proceedings."[221]

After the hundreds of hours Fardella had spent on the case, gathering and collating thousands of emails, he was, understandably, annoyed and just a little sarcastic, responding in an email with subject line, "Colin Mak again brings a shame to Singapore,"

> "More evidence than literally 100s of emails from Colin threatening the life of Leandra Ramm, her family and her autistic brother, which we have already sent?? Certainly difficult to imagine that "further evidence" is needed before further court proceedings can be conducted."[222]

Notwithstanding his irritation, A.J. provided the requested "further evidence," including links to what he called Colin's "recent handiwork done under two new aliases."[223] One was a posting on the notorious "complaintsboard.com" an extortion machine run out of Russia, known for posting inflammatory and defamatory material, only removing it after receiving money to do so.

The other was on blogger, where Colin had adopted a new persona.

Tan, in an attempt to assuage Fardella's fears about Colin having possibly traveled out of the country, assured him,

> "Colin has been diligently reporting to the police station on every Monday without fail and SIO Amirudin had just seen Colin in person about an hour ago in the police station, "

It was time for Fardella to show his trump card:

> "I am happy that Colin is complying with his check ins every Monday, but this is obviously not stopping him from diligently continuing his cyber-violence against many, including me and my family,...I have been added as a new target in retaliation for my efforts to bring peace to Leandra Ramm. "

Fardella hoped that his tactic of shaming Singapore would, along with the "further evidence" convince them to pursue their prosecution of Mak, who, by blogging during Colin's quasi "house arrest" was causing the Singapore Police Force to lose face.

Wish They All Could Be California Cops

Simultaneous to Singapore's renewed interest in my ordeal, *and* independently of it, Fardella began pressing the Mak case with his friend, an FBI Special Agent in Oakland, California. Gordon Jenkins a/k/a "Gordy," had met A.J. as part of a previous investigation, unrelated to the Mak matter. Turns out they had gone to the same elementary school in San Francisco, back in the sixties.

After Singapore arrested, then released Mak, Fardella had hit a wall. Despite Mak's arrest, and *in spite* of the huge packet of cyber evidence compiled at my Brooklyn brownstone back in 2011, the U.S. Attorney had again (informally) refused to take my case.

Like me, A.J. is nothing if not persistent when it comes to something he believes in passionately. He wasn't about to let more than a year of painstaking efforts, lobbying and the success of Colin's arrest slip away from him. He wanted justice for me, he really did. So, he began putting the pressure on Agent Jenkins. This was a historic case and the FBI would look like the good guy—in sharp contrast to the way they looked now—lazy and weak.

While lobbying Gordy, Fardella approached another friend in California law enforcement, veteran homicide detective Ed Sanchez, who'd served on the Pittsburg Police Department for 18 years.

At the urging of Fardella, PPD and the FBI formed a local cooperative case to investigate Mak further. The first order of business was to send the hard evidence (the unopened love letter) to Contra Costa County's crime lab for fingerprint and DNA analysis.

Bag and Tag

In 2011, I fedexed a package of hard evidence to Fardella, a veritable trousseau of gifts from Colin over the years—silk clothes, underwear, some cheap silver-plated jewelry and a letter, never opened with a return address to and postmark from Singapore.

When A.J. got the package, he followed "acceptable scientific methods to "bag and tag" evidence. Before touching the package contents, he donned latex gloves, then videotaped opening the package-- so that the chain of evidentiary custody was transparent and unbroken. Fardella carefully placed the evidence on a pre-designated surface in his Pittsburg forensics lab. Then, following protocol, he photographed each item, electronically "tagging" it, by memorializing the image with metadata, including time and date stamping.

Fardella suspected certain items contained fingerprints and DNA, which would appear under black light after spraying the surface with Luminol. But he was interested less in DNA on the lingerie and more in the unopened letter. A.J. recalled an admonition by his retired Secret Service buddy, Al, the one who had introduced Fardella into the Electronic Crimes Task Force.
"Never ignore the low hanging fruit, A.J."

Hidden in plain sight among the glitter and smut of Colin's mementos was this simple letter and envelope. Fardella was counting on the fact that Mak, ever the elusive predator online, would not be so careful to cover his traces on a three dimensional document. That he most likely handled and licked the envelope. Fardella hoped that Mak's letter would be the low hanging fruit connecting Colin to every one of the emails, texts and blog entries he sent to me or wrote about me.

We crossed our fingers, hoping for a fingerprint.

Lust Letter

The letter that would be Colin's undoing was yet another example of his unhealthily desperate sexuality. The fact that I was reading it for the first time under "safe" conditions didn't lessen the feelings welling up inside me—disgust, shame, and anxiety—the same cocktail of emotions I'd experienced throughout the "at bay" period.

Colin dated the letter March 26, 2010, and wrote on the envelope a return address of 301 River Valley Road, a Victorian home called *Fern Loft,* which rented out rooms and beds for the "lowest rates." I found it curious that the envelope's postmark, March 30, 2010, was the day after I had sent Colin my final email, promising never to communicate with him again, thereby ending the misery that was "at bay."

Silvestra,

> I am angry with you for I have not heard from you in nearly 2 weeks. Your voice and words revitalize me and always this I want you to know. I love you.

> Just how are you doing on the ship I want to know. I am 100 percent jealous of you and 1000 percent wanting to make love to you in every luxury cabin on the ship in the middle of the ocean, totally oblivious to violent raging storms. May our cries of passion overwhelm them all!!!

> I have to make love to you soon my Silvestra. You drive me into the most pleasant state of wild, passionate frenzy.

> I shall be having your most beautiful face in my hands, grabbing your breasts, holding you so tightly for fear of losing you. So tell me you love me and tell me you do care about me.

Tell me my only love, that you want my very hard rod in your warm mouth.

Tell me you want to savor every golden drop of my sacred white elixir.

I need to be loved by you. I need to marry you because every day without you is pure sexual torment. I need to wake up every morning knowing I can give you wild, long and passionate lazy kisses. My heart begs you to surrender .

Love, your Colin

26th March 2010

This letter and envelope would soon be in the FBI's Quantico crime lab, scrutinized by the best forensic scientists in the world.

One Good Man

Fardella had long suspected that there were prints on the "lust" letter postmarked March 29, 2010, the day after I had emailed Mak my final good bye. Unfortunately, Contra Costa County had no exemplar of Colin's fingerprints to compare against, sending back the evidence to Sanchez, with a finding of "inconclusive."

The irony was that Colin's prints *were* in the Homeland Security Database; Mak had submitted fingerprints as a condition to receiving his student visa from the United States. The problem was that Coco County had no access to them. I was understanding, first hand, the need for interoperability among law enforcement agencies, including access to evidence databases by local police.

Undeterred, Fardella again approached FBI special agent Gordon Jenkins. Given the current fingerprint roadblock, and the likelihood that Mak's fingerprints were on the letter and envelope, would Jenkins send the letter to FBI labs in Quantico for analysis?

By now, it was October, 2012. Given the lack of interest by the Manhattan FBI field office, Gordon saying "yes" was tantamount to rebellion; at the very least he'd be sticking his neck out for me. Amazingly, Jenkins agreed. On October 17, 2012, Jenkins forwarded the letter and other evidence to the FBI criminal lab in Quantico, Virginia. My case now had an official FBI Case ID number, and a related Lab Number.

It was hard to believe that it had already been two years since I sent the evidence package to Fardella, and seven years since I'd first "met" (but never actually met) Colin. I realized that Colin had been stalking and harassing me for a quarter of my life. Most crimes are finite— meaning, that a robbery or a mugging, even a murder is usually dispatched in a few moments. But stalking didn't stop; it seemed endless, and hopeless.

Though I'd never met or even communicated with him, I was so grateful to Gordon Jenkins for taking a risk, and doing the right thing.

Game, Set, Fingerprint Match

It was the third week of May, 2013; I had just returned from London, filming a piece with **October Films** about Colin's stalking-- to be aired by *Investigation Discovery* later in the year. I had barely overcome my jet lag when Fardella began pushing me to complete my revised affidavit and have a Singapore Consulate official notarize it. Time was of the essence.

Around the same time, the FBI Laboratory in Quantico had concluded their fingerprint analysis of the love-lust letter-with-envelope and, on June 7, 2013, issued a "Report of Examination" to Oakland, California FBI and Special Agent Jenkins. On June 26, 2013, Gordon called Fardella to tell him the findings. Running their results against prints collected in the Homeland Security database, Quantico found two useable prints belonging to Colin Mak.

Ecstatic, Fardella immediately emailed Sergeant Amirudin, handling the Mak matter in Singapore.

Dear Sergeant,

Just wanted to share the good news that was told to me today by US FBI Special Agent Gordon Jenkins, the results of the finger print work on the envelope associated with exhibit EE, the love letter that was sent to the victim Leandra Ramm through regular postal mail, are in from the FBI crime lab in Quantico, AND there is a positive match on two separate prints to the accused Colin Mak Yew Loong from fingerprints that were obtained from him upon his entry into the United States when he came here as a student.

Currently the report and results are being forwarded back through the chain of custody to SA Jenkins, who will turn that over to Detective Ed Sanchez of the Pittsburg California Police Department, and then back to us. Detective Sanchez and I can go to the Consulate in San Francisco to have this certified and then fedex it to you. At that point I will also certify my affidavit verifying the Exhibits which were sent along with Leandra's affidavit.

FEDEX has stated that you should receive the affidavit and exhibits which Leandra sent from New York this Thursday.

I am pleased of course that we have a match to the accused which ties him physically to this letter and by association to all of the email and other evidence.

A few weeks later, in early July, 2013, I strode confidently into the Singapore Consulate, swore out my affidavit and left with a notarized copy, which I overnighted to Singapore, copy to A.J.

Post Script

On July 9, 2013, Fardella proudly transmitted to Singapore policemen Amirudin and colleague Abdullah, copy to supervisor Eddie Tan, the FBI fingerprint report from Quantico. Although Jenkins had alerted Fardella to the matching prints, Fardella had just then received the report,

Greetings Sergeant Md Amirudin Md Abdullah,

I am pleased to forward to you, courtesy of Pittsburg PD and the FBI, attached to this email an unclassified copy of the results of the fingerprint examination conducted by the FBI lab in Quantico of the letter and envelope which were photographed and submitted to you certified by Singapore Consulate as exhibit EE attached to Leandra's affidavit.

A match was made to Colin on fingerprints found on the envelope of Exhibit EE as is highlighted in the attached report.

It is my understanding that an official transfer of the evidence and all reports will be forwarded to you through the FBI LEGAT in the near future.

Thank You for your efforts in this case and I look forward to hearing from you.

Cheers!

A. J. Fardella[224]

Thanks to A.J.'s encouraging the FBI to take my case seriously, Singapore will have a tough time trying to wriggle out of prosecuting Colin. And the FBI, like it or not, is in it for the long haul. We will see.

In the meantime, I'll relish my hard-won peace. And I did win. It doesn't matter whether Colin rears his head again—I won and made a dent in the enormous fight against cyber stalking. I am at peace, and I am enjoying my life—singing, performing and savoring my newfound freedom.

EPILOGUE

A Letter to My Tormentor

Colin,

We've never met, but your emails have revealed to me who you really are, because in them I've spotted patterns, Colin, and have made some pretty reasonable deductions about you, your personality, your soft spots.

Your excessive correspondence to me allowed me to look into your soul.

One of the things I keep pondering is how I let you get so deeply in my consciousness, without ever having seen or met you. The Italians call a nightmare an *incubo*, which literally means "in a cube." I imagine the metaphor of being trapped in a cube with you; that's how I feel about the virtual world you created—trapped and frightened. Being in-cubed with you has taught me a lot about how to dissect an email from you.

I know you only by the identities you have intended for me to see. These identities weren't finished products, and you never keep in character for long, so ultimately Colin comes shining through. I wondered whether you ever really wanted to disguise who you are. I think that you wanted *me* to recognize that it is always you, Colin, behind the identities—thousands of identities. Like snowflakes, these email addresses shared the attributes of numerosity and yet each slightly unique, the identities sharing more similarities to one another than differences. And they all pointed back to you. Which, I suspect, was always intentional.

You wanted this to be our little joke, an acknowledgment by me that you were behind all of the emails, that you were so powerful, you could fool people. You wanted me to see how easy it was for you to smother me with messages. You wanted to show me who was boss—

certainly not the men I chose to date. How could I ever fight back against the power you demonstrated?

I suspect for the real Colin, the virtual world was a perfectly controlled environment, where Colin would be recognized for superior intellect, military prowess, general superiority, and artistic prowess.

You've taught me that reality is relative, but that violence and hatred are real, under any façade.

You seemed to have had a very cultured background, quoting philosophers, musicians, and historical facts. I suspect you had some musical training of your own, maybe as a young boy? You liked to tell me what a disappointing career I've had, how my peers had far surpassed me, that I was especially a disappointment because of my genius foundations.

But, what of your own wasted potential, Colin? You have so many true gifts ... multilingual, cultured, educated, and convincing. If only you had had the confidence to pursue a real-world life with these talents, instead of using them to obfuscate, bully, and control.

Get help.

Although I will never understand you, I have managed to forgive you. I have managed to let go of my anger toward you and heal myself. Holding on to the anger was only hurting me. I am at peace with the case now. I am at peace with you.

One of the ways I was able to win was praying for your happiness. We are all one and all connected. I have released you from my life and let you go. I know you are mentally unwell, and I hope that you are able to be healed from your inner prison. I was able to escape from that prison, and I pray you will one day, too.

Your survivor,

Leandra

STALKING A DIVA

Leandra's Thank You

How do I even begin to thank everyone for making this book possible? To have my life story told in a book is a dream come true—a vision manifested into reality. I have many people to thank for that. First and foremost, I would like to thank D. Rocca for her time, passion, and work. Without her, my story would never have been told on paper and certainly not as artfully. She made my story make sense. I would like to thank A.J. Fardella, Data Forensics Expert at Black Diamond Data LLC, for his crucial involvement in my journey from victim to victor. A.J. works tirelessly and passionately, all the while fighting for justice.

Thank you to my immediate family: Adrienne Ramm, David Ramm, Courtney Ramm, and Logan Ramm. Thank you, Mom and Dad, for bringing me into this world despite all odds. Thank you for giving me love, confidence, a wonderful happy home, the conviction that I can overcome all obstacles, and nurturing my passion to go after my dreams. Thank you, Courtney, for being my little sister and looking up to me, teaching me things I have never known and in turn, giving me a little sister to look up to. Thank you, Logan, for teaching me that happiness is an internal state of being, especially in the midst of huge challenges.

Thank you to all my other family members for their consistent love and support. A special thanks to my Great-aunt Evelyn Margulies for her wonderful stories of my ancestors.

I would like to thank Monroe Mann, Dustin Bear, Carelle Flores, Jim Coniglio, October Films and Investigation Discovery, and all of the many friends and colleagues who are in or have been in my life.

Lastly, a big thank you to the multi-universe for providing me with the many obstacles that I discovered I can overcome. I am grateful for everything that is presented to me. I embrace my victories, struggles, and all my experiences, from fright, to fight, to flight ... it is all a precious gift.

Leandra Ramm

August 1, 2012
New York

About Leandra Ramm

Leandra Ramm is a versatile singer and actress with an "extraordinary voice" (Anderson Cooper). Leandra has performed at Carnegie Hall, Lincoln Center, Symphony Space, La MaMa, and 59E59 Theaters among other venues. In addition to being a lead vocalist on Celebrity Cruises, Leandra has performed with numerous theater and opera companies throughout the world. Her favorite roles performed include *The Full Monty* (Estelle) at The Media Theatre, *Iolanthe* (Leila) at The Buxton Opera House (UK), *Mario and The Magician* (Silvestra) with Center for Contemporary Opera, *Man of la Mancha* (Antonia) with Diablo Theater Company, and *The Endless Road* by Kurt Weill (soloist) with The American Symphony Orchestra. In addition to many previous television appearances, Leandra stars in an episode of the new Lifetime Television series, "My Life Is A Lifetime Movie". The program features cinematic re-creations and first-person interviews with women in peril who recount their experiences that are said to be so unbelievable that they must be true. She is also featured in an upcoming one hour Investigation Discovery series, filmed in London and tentatively titled, "Obsessed" about her ordeal. Leandra is excited to share her life story and unbelievable cyber-stalking experience on this groundbreaking show.

Leandra has also released many albums, all available on iTunes, Amazon, and CDbaby.com. This is Leandra's first book, and she is thrilled to work with D. Rocca. For more information, please visit http://www.leandraramm.com.

About D. Rocca

D. Rocca was born in Long Island, New York. An author and privacy attorney, she practices under her maiden name and lives in the San Francisco Bay Area with her family.

Stalking a Diva is her first nonfiction work.

ACKNOWLEDGEMENTS

The Publisher and Authors would like to gratefully recognize (in no particular order):

Families: Tanner, Ramm, Fardella, Della Rocca; Interns: Miranda Claggette, Christian Talavera, Chris Sims; Friends, Colleagues, Other Great People & Organizations : Al Lewis, Alexis Bowater, Ryan Hale, Tom Galligan, Dave Chaney, Detective Ed Sanchez, Pittsburg Police, Pittsburg Police Chief Brian Addington, Oakland Office of the FBI, San Francisco USSS Electronic Crimes Task Force, Pittsburg California Police Force, Contra Costa County Office of Sheriff Forensic Services Division, FBI Criminal Science Laboratory Biometric Services Division, Quantico, Virginia, Singapore Police Force Clementi Division, International Programs Division of the USSS in Singapore, The Economist, The Bay Area News Group, Robert Solanga, Mark Albertson, Tom LaFleur, Ron Shirley, Lucky Woo, Martin Dunn, Monroe Mann, Dustin Bear, Jim Coniglio, Robert and Tun Ormiston, FBI Special Agent Gordon Jenkins, Fix-That Mac, October Films and Investigation Discovery.

For more information and to share your insights

into 'Stalking A Diva' please visit:

https://stalkingadiva.com

APPENDIX A

ECONOMIST QUESTIONS AND ANSWERS TO LEANDRA RAMM, MARCH 31, 2011

On Thu, Mar 31, 2011 at 6:01 <AMXXX> wrote:

Dear Leandra,

Thank you so much for agreeing to do this. There are a few questions below, but do feel free to add extra points that I haven't thought of!

1. What is your own experience of cyberstalking?

2. What did you do about it?

3. What assistance have you had from both legal bodies and from agencies (such as NSS) with your experience of this crime?

4. Do you think that cyberstalking is well understood at the moment?

5. Do you think it is well policed?

6. What do you think should happen to improve the situation?

7. How has it affected your life?

All the very best,

On Wed, Apr 6, 2011 at 7:07 PM, Leandra Ramm <leandraramm>☐ wrote☐☐☐☐☐
Hi XXXX,

Please see my answers below. Thank you!

1. What is your own experience of cyberstalking?

It has been a nightmare! I have been cyberstalked for about 5 years now by a man that I have never met and who saw me on TV. I am a singer and entertainer. I was on TV on CNN in

2005, which aired internationally. A man that lives in Singapore saw me and latched on. This man claimed he Googled my name to find where I was working at the time. He then called an opera company where I was working and said he saw me on TV and that he was the producer of a music festival in Singapore. The opera company thought he sounded legitimate and gave me his contact information. He definitely did sound legitimate and was very convincing. I unfortunately found out he was not the director of a Singapore music festival, but only until after I sent him my resumé, headshot, and demo DVD which had all of my personal information on it such as my physical address, email address, phone number, and all my work and school history.

I got the red flags that something was wrong and he was not who he said he was. This man started to want to have long phone conversations, emails, IM chats, etc. I turned down a relationship with this man and told him to "cease and desist." He has ever since been trying to make my daily life impossible. He emails me, my friends, family, colleagues, companies I work for, and anyone associated with me that he can find on the Internet. He sends death threats, bomb threats, and multiple types of disturbing emails multiple times daily! He even used identity theft to create a fake email, pretending he was me, and emailed my manager saying I no longer wanted to be on their roster. They believed it and thought it was me. I only found out after going on my manager's website and noticing I was no longer there.

He has multiple email addresses with aliases and uses these to stalk me and everyone I know. He created a terrible blog about me which says absolutely untrue and ridiculous statements which harm my reputation such as, "here are more pictures of Leandra Ramm the runaway criminal—report her whereabouts to FBI for grand theft of 40 000 USD immediately," and "Leandra emails sponsor—sex in exchange for emergency cash—a total whore," and "Leandra Ramm posing for the webcam for her sponsor tell us what you think." As I am a singer, I am on many online websites about my vocal career and my latest songs and albums. He comments on Internet posts about me saying slanderous, defamatory things. He copied my videos on YouTube and reposted them under his YouTube account, saying slanderous things such as I am an international criminal. He created Facebook hate groups about me, and countless other means of online stalking. He also uses physical mail and the telephone to stalk me. I know this man's identity now, Colin Mak Yew Loong of Singapore.

2. What did you do about it?

The first thing I did, when I started to receive death threats, pictures of guns and threats to the companies I was working, was I went to the FBI in New York City. I brought all the evidence I had and was assigned a detective. After a couple of weeks of the detective doing investigation, he told me to "just ignore the emails; they are out of the FBI's jurisdiction."

I then went to the New York Police Department; they had a similar response. They said they cannot help me because the emails are coming from Singapore. Then I went to the Singapore Police. I filed an electronic police report twice, I spoke to officers on the phone, emailed them and they said it is a "nonarrestable" offense and... the police will also not be conducting further investigation into the matter. ...Nevertheless, please be assured that should Ms. Ramm feel an immediate threat to her life or safety whilst she is in Singapore, she may call the police hotline '999' and police resources will provide her with immediate assistance."

I also hired a private investigator in Singapore and in the USA and a lawyer. I contacted the Singapore Embassy in Washington, D.C., the United Nations, the American Embassy in Singapore. They all said there is nothing they can do or never got back to me. I reported the blog to Blogger and they did not take it down because "Blogger does not remove allegedly defamatory, libelous, or slanderous material from Blogger.com or BlogSpot.com. If a contact email address is listed on the blog, we recommend you working directly with the author to have the content in question removed or changed."

I also reported the threatening emails to all of the stalker's email providers, they did nothing. I tried blocking the emails (which in Gmail means the emails go to your trash) and changing my email. He just found my new email address and harassed even more the email addresses he did have: my family, friends, colleagues, and companies where I work.

When I felt I exhausted my resources, I went to the press to try to get my story out there in the public eye. Amazingly, when an American newspaper told my story about cyberstalking, it was then removed because the reporter was getting threats of being "beaten up and raped" unless the article was pulled. The reporter said. "Yes, his intimidating tactics won. I'm sorry."

There are unfortunately no laws for International cyberstalking yet, so there is really not much I can do. It has really been an awful experience. I am very frustrated because nothing can be done says all the authorities. The USA authorities say it is out of their jurisdiction and the Singapore Police say it is out of their jurisdiction...so it's in no one's jurisdiction!

3. What assistance have you had from both legal bodies and from agencies (such as NSS) with your experience of this crime?

In addition to what I mentioned above, I went to cyber crime websites for help. They all were shocked at my situation and just recommended "ignoring the stalker,", "blocking the emails," and "reporting the emails to the ISP of the sender." (These are all things that I already was doing and my situation still persisted). NSS (http://www.nss.org.uk) has been the most helpful in my situation! I was pleasantly surprised when Chief Executive Alexis Bowater reached out to me and went out of her way to find help for me in my situation. She contacted different authorities and really helped in my emotional well-being as well as trying to find solutions. I am unfortunately still being cyberstalked, but I found a safe haven in NSS to go to for help

4. Do you think that cyber-stalking is well understood at the moment?

No, I do not! I believe people have no clue how damaging cyberstalking can be and do not understand it at all. Cyberstalking has affected my emotional well-being, my social activities, my career, my work ... everything! Imagine getting death threats on a daily basis and having your friends, family, coworkers, and boss all getting death threats as long as they are associated with you. I feel humiliated, helpless, and abused, and all they can say is "just ignore it, there is nothing that can be done."

I believe one day in the future we will all look back in awe that people were allowed to get away with stalking on the Internet. The Internet is one world, separated by nothing.

5. Do you think it is well policed?

No, I do not! I was amazed that the authorities could not help me. They think email threats and cyberstalking are nothing. They think they have bigger fish to fry. The Internet, however, is becoming more and more part of our daily life. Stalking on the Internet is just as bad, if not worse, than real-life physical stalking. You can't put a restraining order on an international cyberstalker. The police don't want to help, and there are no laws for this. It is quite amazing. I have felt as I was part of the twilight zone going through this experience. When I tell people nothing can be done, they can't believe it either.

6. What do you think should happen to improve the situation?

I think a law urgently needs to be passed about cyberstalking. No matter what country you live in, or where in the world someone is stalking another online, it should be a punishable offense. There should be an international law passed that makes cyberstalking illegal no matter where you are. The different police departments of each country should work together on this international law. If a person is found stalking someone on the Internet, they should be located through their IP address and then physically arrested for the crime. A lifetime restraining order should be put in place between the two parties, both physically and on the Internet. The cyberstalker's Internet usage should be limited if not abolished all together. One day we will get there. The Internet is so new, however, this hasn't happened yet.

7. How has it affected your life?

This has affected my life so much. I can only imagine what my life would be without my cyberstalker. I live in the USA and I am a free citizen living in a free country, yet I feel trapped and I feel no peace. I am scared for my safety.

My career has been affected as people don't want the liability of working with me because of this. My online reputation is damaged because the stalker has put so much defamation and slander about me online. My personal relationships have suffered because I am under so much stress because of this and people's opinions of me have changed, some people think it's my fault. My social activities, hobbies, and things I used to do for fun and enjoy have been limited. Everything in my life has changed because of this. As a singer trying to build a career, this has been damaging. As a woman, this has been damaging. As a free person and human being, this has been damaging.

DISCUSSION POINTS—
Book Club

Survey Says...

If you believe that I am alone in being the victim of cyberstalking, I urge you to perform your own random sampling of both male and female friends, colleagues, relatives or acquaintances, your daughters, sons, mothers, fathers, aunts, uncles, sisters, and brothers. If you are of an age group that doesn't remember a time before computers, and you are a female, it is likely that you have been cyberstalked or cyberbullied. Preposterous? Not at all, depending on your definition of these terms. And since there's no consistent definition, it's time we identify it, label it, and expose it because it is a cancer that is destroying the confidence and morale of women and girls worldwide.

So, next time there's a group of you girls and women together, get the answers to these questions. The important thing is to open this subject to real discussion and debate, to remove the shame and guilt many women feel about being stalked and bullied and, eventually, to change law enforcement's trend of victimizing the victim. [Comment: the new rape)

1.   How many times have you received unwanted attention in an email, text mail, on Facebook or other social media?

2.   Before today, whom, if anyone, have you told?

3.   Have you contacted law enforcement? If not, why not? If so, what was the result?

4.   How have you dealt with these communications? Have you: closed down your social media (e.g., Facebook) accounts,

changed your phone number, changed your identity, or done nothing at all?

5. How does being pursued make you feel?

    a. It's your fault for posting online

    b. You try to ignore it, but know it's there

    c. You feel anxious

    d. You feel scared

    e. You feel depressed

    f. You feel alone

    g. You feel like no one takes you seriously

    h. You've tried to tell your husband, boyfriend, brother, and they told you that you were exaggerating

    i. You have nightmares, feel sick, or are unable to relax

    j. You fear for your safety

Now ask these questions of the men in your life, same demographic, meaning they use social media, they text, email and so on. See how they respond.

INDEX

[1] Affidavit of Leandra Ramm, Submitted to USSS Electronic Crimes Task Force International Programs Division, August 10, 2011.

[2] Throughout this book, "father," "Dad" and other references to paternity, unless otherwise specific to Donor Clear, will refer to David Ramm, the only father I've ever known.

[3] Interview with Robert Graham, *Eugenics Bulletin*, Winter 1983.

[4] Ibid.

[5] Ibid.

[6] http://en.wikipedia.org/wiki/The_Phil_Donahue_Show

[7] http://en.wikipedia.org/wiki/Hero_and_Leander

[8] According to Plotz's *The Genius Factory*, Fuchsia sired many more than 10 children—somewhere in the dozens.

[9] Stormo Rochalie screenshot from Blogger.com, December 26, 2011.

[10] Harvard University Police Department Flyer— Information.

[11] This article, by veteran crime reporter Robert Salonga, described the work A.J. had done on my case.

[12] Excerpt from chat with Colin M 2010 02-14.

[13] Email excerpt from Colin M warbird5k to Leandra Erin Ramm, Monday, August 30, 2010.

[14] Affidavit of Leandra Ramm, August 10, 2011.

[15] Email from warbird5k, May 12, 2006.

[16] Email from warbird5k, April 18, 2006.

[17] Email from warbird5k, June 25, 2006.

[18] Email from Leandra Ramm to warbird5k, June 25, 2006.

[19] Email from warbird5k, February 10, 2006.

[20] "Allegro Con Brio" is a reference from Beethoven's Symphony Number 5, I. Allegro Con Brio.

[21] Lori Singer, also a renowned cellist, co-starred in the original *Footloose, The Falcon and the Snowman*, and other well-known films.

[22] Colin Mak (warbird5k) email of April 28, 2006, reads: "By the time you read this—I would have sent you a present—a little something from Chanel to Gregory's violin shop...collect it there.
I am "forcing" you to meet him...heh heh
—Colin MaK
"So Long As the Human Spirit Thrives on This Planet, Music

in Some Living Form Will accompany And Sustain It and Give It Expressive Meaning."—Aaron Copeland.

23 Email from Mikelee70, January 14, 2007.

24 Email from Tony Thille, January 14, 2007.

25 Email from Colin Mak to Leandra Ramm, January 14, 2007.

26 Email from Mikelee70 Mikelee To: warbird5k warbird5k

27 Singapore Customs Press Release, October 11, 2006.

28 The real Tony Thille was an associate of Colin's in a Swedish company, Protec Consulting, and was involved with Colin in an international weapons-dealing case, the first of its kind tried in Singapore.

29 Email from warbird5k to <Redacted>

30 Email from warbird5k to <Redacted>

31 Chaandrran was Colin's co-defendant in the Singapore case.

32 Email from Tony Thille, January 14, 2007.

33 As with all emails concerning this case, unless independently verified or collaborated, Thille's email correspondence could have been genuine or could have been spoofed.

34 Letter from Colin Mak to AG Office, March 21, 2006.

35 Email from Colin Mak to <Redacted>.

36 From Colin Mak to <Redacted>

37 Michael Wade Lee, my former boyfriend.

38 Email from Colin Mak to Michael Wade Lee, 2007.

39 Email from Colin Mak meteorpacifico, Subject: death to Michael Wade Lee at any price, June 7, 2007.

40 Affidavit of Leandra Ramm, August 10, 2011.

41 Email from Jasmine Carerra to Jim Shaeffer, June 25, 2007.

42 Email from Jim Shaeffer to Leandra Ramm, June 25, 2007.

43 Email from Colin Mak to Frank Tobias <veritas 30> to Leandra Ramm, Dec 12, 2009, 7:51 pm.

44 Email from Mona Hanson to Colin Mak, December, 2007.

45 Email from Mona Hanson to Colin Mak, December, 2007.

46 Email from Mona Hanson to Colin Mak, December, 2007.

47 Excerpt from ChatwithColinM200900905.

48 Shakespeare, Hamlet—Polonius.

49 Mainguard International Investigations Report #20059073.

50 NCVC.org

51 Email from Mona Hanson to Colin Mak dated December , 2007.

52 Email from MIGGY MIGGY! spicekits130, dated October 30, 2007.

53 Chat with Colin M2009 09-28

54 Email from Colin M warbird5k to Leandra Ramm, subject

line "Silvestra, Birkles the Cat," May 17, 2009.

[55] Email of Colin M warbird5k, subject line "cheer up Birkles!", January 6, 2010.

[56] Photos of Colin Mak, Book of Evidence, © 2011, 2012, Black Diamond Data, LLC.

[57] Email from Colin MaKwarbird5k to Leandra Ramm, January 20, 2008, 12:15 AM.

[58] Dictionary.com

[59] Email from MIGGH MIGGY spicekits130, pics from HK, September 6, 2007.

[60] Mainguard International Investigations Report 20059073CMSG.

[61] Mona Hanson talked about sending Colin to a psychiatrist in Hong Kong.

[62] Email from Colin Mak to Leandra Ramm, dated May 18, 2009, 8:55 AM (Colin M. collection).

[63] Email from Colin Mak to Leandra Ramm dated June 9, 2009, 9:13 AM.

[64] Email excerpt from Colin M <warbird5k>, subject "your intimates," March 8, 2010 8:09 PM.

[65] ChatwithColinM 2009 09-05

[66] ChatwithColinM 2009 09-05

[67] Just to name some of the more prevalent personas, there was miggymiggy and multiple variations on that name, such as miggymiggy90, stormo rochalie, sopranogirl, jannbrahmos, jasmine cardozi, colin mak, spicekits, and veritas.

[68] Email from Miggy Miggy spieckits130, September 13, 2007.

[69] Email from April Mendez vertias30.

[70] Email excerpt from Colin M warbird5k, subject, "today," February 16, 2010, 1:12 AM.

[71] Email excerpt from Colin M warbird5k, subject, TO THE ONES MADE BY IN VITRO;) CHEERS!, October 4, 2010, 4:14 AM.

[72] Email from Colin MaK warbird5k to Leandra Ramm, January 13, 2008.

[73] Email from Colin M warbird5k to Adrienne And David Ramm Rammda, Leandra Ramm leandraramm, Fri, Jul 30, 2010, at 2:42 AM.

[74] Email excerpt from Stormo Silvestra <stormorsilvestra> to Leandra Ramm <leandraramm>, Adrienne and David Ramm <rammda>, Courtney Mighan Ramm <courtneyramm>, Gale Martin <galemartin09> Mike Hogan <mhogan80>, Mon, May 23, 2011, at 7:51 AM.

[75] Email excerpt from Miggy MIggy <miggymiggy90>, March 22, 2011, 7:33 AM

[76] Email subject line from Colin M <warbid5k> to Leandra Ramm <LeandraRamm>, copies to David Plotz

<david.plot>, Adrienne and David Ramm <rammda>, Courtney Mighan Ramm <courtneyramm>, Mike Hogan <mhogan80>, August 26, 2011, 8:22 AM.

[77] Email from Colin M warbird5k to Leandra Ramm, Wed., Jul 21, 2010, 3:00 AM.

[78] Email from Colin M warbird5k to Leandra Ramm, Wed., Jul 21, 2010, 3:00 AM.

[79] Email excerpt from Colin M <warbird5k2> to Adrienne and David Ramm ,Courtney Ramm ,Leandra Erin Ramm

[80] Email excerpt from Colin M <warbird5k> to Leandra Ramm <leandraramm>, Sun, Aug 8, 2010, 10:56 PM.

[81] *Untermensch:* German for underman, subman, subhuman; plural: *Untermenschen* is a term that became infamous when the Nazi racial ideology used it to describe "inferior people," especially "the masses from the East," that is, Jews, Gypsies, Poles, along with other Slavic people like the Russians, Serbs, Belarusians and Ukrainians."

[82] Chat with Colin M 2009 08-21.

[83] Chat with Colin M 2009 09-28.

[84] Email from Stormorochalie to Nataliya Zapolina dated May 16, 2010, forwarded to Leandra Ramm.

[85] Chat with Colin M 2009,09-28.

[86] Email from Frank Tobias (aka Colin) to Darrin from Diablo Valley Opera Company.

[87] Email from Miggy Miggy to <ana>, dated February 24, 2010.

[88] "I think, therefore I am," in French :"Je pense, donc je suis," a philosophical proposal by writer, philosopher, and mathematician René Descartes (31 March 1596 – 11 February 1650).

[89] DivasGoneWild.blogspot.com, August 5, 2011, 4:20 PM.

[90] Affidavit of Leandra Ramm, U.S. Secret Service Electronic Crime Task Force International Programs Division, August 10, 2011, paragraph 28.

[91] Email from Miggy M <spicekits> to Michael Wade Lee, April 7, 2007.

[92] Email from gilder, robert to Leandra Ramm, April 10, 2009.

[93] Email excerpt from MIGGY! spciekits130 to Michael Wade Lee, copies to Leandraopera, leandraramm, leandraramm, courtneyramm, Rammda, becky, sam, Cathy, Barnaby.

[94] Email excerpt from Miggy MIggy miggymiggy90 to Dustin Bear bearsax, cc: leandraramm, leandraramm 2, David and Adrienne Ramm rammda, court Neyramm, Michael Wade Lee, Tue, Aug 17, 2010 at 12:40 AM.

[95] Email from Colin M warbird5k to Leandra Erin Ramm , Mon Aug 16, 2010, at 11:31 PM.

[96] Email from Colin Mai to David Ram, June 6, 2007.

[97] Email from Stormo Rochalie to Adrienne and David

Ramm, copies to others, Friday, July 30, 2010, at 10:35 PM.
[98] Fax excerpt from evidence package submitted by Black Diamond Data, LLC, to Singapore Police, November 7, 2011.
[99] Email excerpt from Stormo Rochalie to Leandra Ramm, March 24, 2011, 9:46 PM PDT. Subject: Leandra Ramm's Sister Courtney Ramm and autistic brother Logam Ramm to be beaten.
[100] Email from Stormo Rochalie to Leandra Ramm, others copied, July 30, 2010, at 10:38 AM.
[101] Email excerpt from Stormo Rochalie to Leandra Ramm, others copied, March 24, 2011, at 9:35:44 PM PDT.
[102] Email from Stormo Rochalie, Saturday, May 7, 2011, at 10:38 AM to Adrienne and David Ramm, copies to David Plotz, Heidi Beckman, Courtney Mighan Ramm, Leandra Ramm.
[103] Email from Colin M warbird5k, Sunday, May 15, 2011, at 5:25 AM to Leandra Erin Ramm, copies to Adrienne and David Ramm, copies to David Plotz, Heidi Beckman, Courtney Mighan Ramm, Leandra Ramm.
[104] Email from Colin Mak to Leandra Ramm, dated April 3, 2009.
[105] Email from Colin Mak to Leandra Ramm, dated May 7, 2009, 12:09 AM (Colin M collection)
[106] Email from Leandra Ramm, dated May 11, 2009, to Colin Mak.
[107] Email from Colin M warbird5k, to Adrienne and David Ramm, Leandra Erin Ramm, Courtney Ramm, Dustin Bear, Friday, July 30, 2010, 3:15 AM.
[108] Email from Colin M warbird5k, to Leandra Erin Ramm, Friday, July 30, 2010, 3:24 AM.
[109] Email from Colin M warbird5k, some pics of HK, March 8, 2008.
[110] Mainguard International Report citing Hong Kong case details.
[111] Email from Leandra Ramm to judiciary.gov.hk, dated March 25, 2010.
[112] Email from enquiry@ judiciary.gov.hk to Leandra Ramm, May 11, 2010, at 3:15 AM.
[113] Elle.com.hk
[114] Email from Colin M warbird5k to Leandra Ramm, forwarding email from miggymiggy90 to SKYE Boutique, February 24, 2010.
[115] Email from SKYE Boutique to miggymiggy90, February 24, 2010.
[116] Email from SKYE Boutique to miggymiggy90, February 24, 2010.
[117] Email from Stormo Rochalie to Nataliya Zapolina, May 16, 2010.
[118] www.exporters.sg/member_profile.asp?co_id=51090

[119] Email from Mona Hanson to Leandra Ramm, December 6, 2007.

[120] Email extract from Mona Hanson to Leandra Ramm, December 8, 2007, 4:12 AM.

[121] Email from Mona Hanson to Colin Mak/Miggy Miggy, December 7, 2007, 7:03 AM.

[122] Email from jdpdindc, May 1, 2005.

[123] Email excerpt from Colin M to Leandra Ramm, March 15, 2008, 3:10 AM.

[124] Letter from Colin Mak to Silvestra (Leandra Ramm) hand delivered with flowers by Brian Asparro, July 30, 2010.

[125] Affidavit of Leandra Ramm, USSS Electronic Crime Task Force International Programs Division, August 10, 2011.

[126] Proverbs 28:1.

[127] *The Genius Factory*, David Plotz, 2005.

[128] Excerpts: email from Leandra Ramm to David Plotz, January 26, 2007, 7:42 PM, from Evidence Package, Black Diamond Data, LLC.

[129] Excerpt of email from David Plotz to Leandra Ramm, January 29, 2007, 11:37 AM.

[130] Email from David Plotz to Leandra Ramm, April 25, 2007, 11:04 AM.

[131] Email from David Plotz to Leandra Ramm, April 25, 2007, 11:04 AM.

[132] Email from Leandra Ramm to David Plotz, April 26, 2007, 12:49 AM.

[133] Email from David Plotz to Leandra Ramm, April 26, 2007, 8:21 AM.

[134] Affidavit of Leandra Ramm to USSS and Singapore Police, August 10, 2011.

[135] Email from Michael Lee to Leandra Ramm; newyork@fbi.gov, Subject: Fwd: FW;HI American OPERA PROJECTS, Date, Tue. May 22, 2007, 5:57 PM.

[136] Email from Leandra Ramm to David Plotz, May 5, 2007, 11:30 PM.

[137] Email from David Plotz to Leandra Ramm, April 27, 2007, 7:57 AM.

[138] Email from <no-reply@ic3.gov> to Leandra Ramm, May 5, 2007.

[139] Email from <no-reply@ic3.gov> to Leandra Ramm, May 5, 2007.

[140] Email from <no-reply@ic3.gov> to Leandra Ramm, May 5, 2007.

[141] Excerpt of email to David Plotz from Leandra Ramm, May 8, 2007, 1:53 PM.

[142] Email from Leandra Ramm to David Plotz, May 8, 2007.

[143] Affidavit of Leandra Ramm to USSS Electronic Crime Task Force, International Programs Division, August 10, 2011.

[144] Email from Leandra Ramm to David Plotz, May 8, 2007, 1:53 PM.

[145] Email from Leandra Ramm to David Plotz, May 15, 2007, Subject: Stalker Situation.

[146] Email from David Plotz to Leandra Ramm, May 15, 2007.

[147] Email from Leandra Ramm to David Plotz, May 20, 2007, 12:20 AM.

[148] Email from Leandra Ramm to David Plotz and Nels Nordquist, May 21, 2007.

[149] Email from Nels Nordquist to Leandra Ramm, May 21, 2007.

[150] Affidavit of Leandra Ramm, Submitted to USSS Electronic Crime Task Force, International Programs Division.

[151] Affidavit of Leandra Ramm, paragraph 12.

[152] Affidavit of Leandra Ramm, Submitted to USSS Electronic Crime Task Force, International Programs Division, paragraph 14.

[153] Michael Wade Lee, my previous boyfriend, also referred to as "MWL."

[154] Email from Colin Mak to Martina Arroyo Foundation, June 22, 2007.

[155] Affidavit of Leandra Ramm, Submitted to USSS Electronic Crime Task Force, International Programs Division, paragraph 13.

[156] Affidavit of Leandra Ramm, Submitted to USSS Electronic Crime Task Force, International Programs Division, paragraph 13.

[157] Affidavit of Leandra Ramm, Submitted to USSS Electronic Crime Task Force, International Programs Division, paragraph 13.

[158] The abbreviation "IM" stands for "Instant messaging"

[159] Affidavit of Leandra Ramm, Submitted to USSS Electronic Crime Task Force, International Programs Division, paragraph 13.

[160] Chat log between Colin Mak warbird5k and Leandra Ramm, August 21, 2009.

[161] Chat log between Colin Mak warbird5k and Leandra Ramm, August 21, 2009.

[162] Affidavit of Leandra Ramm, Submitted to USSS Electronic Crime Task Force, International Programs Division, paragraph 13.

[163] Affidavit of Leandra Ramm, Submitted to USSS Electronic Crime Task Force, International Programs Division, paragraph 13.

[164] Chat log between Colin Mak warbird5k and Leandra Ramm, August 21, 2009.

[165] Affidavit of Leandra Ramm, Submitted to USSS Electronic Crime Task Force, International Programs Division, August 10, 2011, paragraph 14.

[166] Excerpt from chat with Colin M 20100202.

[167] Email from Colin Mak to Leandra Ramm, February 12, 2010, 7:37 PM. Subject: See You at 10:15 AM 15th February.

[168] Affidavit of Leandra Ramm, Submitted to USSS Electronic Crime Task Force, International Programs Division.

[169] Email from Colin Mak to Leandra Ramm, February 15, 2010. Subject: Your size and color La Senza! Silvestra the naughty—now showing!!!!

[170] Affidavit of Leandra Ramm, Submitted to USSS Electronic Crime Task Force, International Programs Division, August 10, 2011, paragraph 28.

[171] TheFreeDictionary.com

[172] Email from Leandra Ramm to Dustin Bear, March 15, 2010.

[173] Email from Leandra Ramm to Dustin Bear, March 22, 2010.

[174] Affidavit of Leandra Ramm, Submitted to USSS Electronic Crime Task Force, International Programs Division, August 10, 2011, paragraph 18.

[175] Email from Leandra Ramm to Colin

[176] Email from Colin M warbird5k to Leandra Ramm, March 29, 2010, 2:44 AM. Subject: Silvestra, FORGIVE—lets talk nicely—please read—please please...FORGIVE ME> I have done you very very very much wrong. Please forgive me.;(

[177] Email chain between Rebecca Marks and Dustin Bear, May 10, 2010.

[178] Email chain between Rebecca Marks and Dustin Bear, May 10, 2010.

[179] Email from Dustin Bear to Rebecca Marks, May 10, 2010.

[180] Email from Dustin Bear to Colin Mak warbird5k, May 21, 2010, 3:31 PM.

[181] Email from Dustin Bear to Colin Mak (posing as carinascott). Copies to MiGGY!, Colin M warbird5k, Frank Tobias, MiGGY, MiGGY MIGGY, Stormo Rochalie, warbird9k, Leandra Ramm, cintiafurtado, mhogan.

[182] Email from Igor Pishun (Colin Mak) to Dustin Bear, November 30, 2010.

[183] Email from Colin M warbird5k, October 27, 2010, 8:18 PM. Subject: A CURSE ON YOU DUSTIN BEAR!

[184] Email from Stormo Rochalie to Leandra Ramm, July 23, 2010, 10:48 AM.

[185] Email from Colin M warbird5k to Leandra Ramm, October 19, 2010, 7:41 AM. Subject—sex.

[186] Email from Colin M warbird5k, November 9, 2010.

[187] Email from Colin M warbird5k, June 30, 2010, 6:05 AM.

[188] Email from Colin M warbird5k, June 30, 2010, 11:24 PM.

[189] Email from Colin M warbird5k, April 28, 2009, 9:59 AM.

[190] Email from Stormo Rochalie to Leandra Ramm, July 23,

2010, 2:26 AM.
[191] Email from Stormo Rochalie to Leandra Ramm, July 23, 2010, 3:58 AM.
[192] Email from Colin M warbird5k to Leandra Ramm, June 30, 2010, 5:18 AM.
[193] Email from Colin M warbird5k to Leandra Ramm, June 30, 2010, 5:28 AM.
[194] Email from Colin M warbird5k to Courtney Ramm, July 30, 2010, 5:29 AM.
[195] Email from Colin M warbird5k to Leandra Erin Ramm, july 28, 2010, 3:52 AM.
[196] Email from Colin M warbird5k to Adrienne and David Ramm, Leandra Erin Ramm, Courtney Ramm, copy to Gale Martin, August 5, 2010.
[197] Affidavit of Leandra Ramm, Submitted to USSS Electronic Crime Task Force, International Programs Division, August 10, 2011, paragraph 30.
[198] Email from SPF Electronic Police Centre to Leandra Ramm.
[199] Affidavit of Leandra Ramm, Submitted to USSS Electronic Crime Task Force, International Programs Division, August 10, 2011, paragraph 30.
[200] Email from SPF Customer Relations Branch, April 11, 2010, 9:10 PM.
[201] Email from Leandra Ramm to Sin Con WAS, May 10, 2010.
[202] Email from SPF Singapore ACS to Leandra Ramm, May 10, 2010, 11:37 PM.
[203] Email from SPF Singapore Embassy representative to Leandra Ramm, Mejar Singh Gill, Counsellor (Admin & Consular) May 11, 2010.
[204] Email from Ponno Kalastree, Managing Director, Mainguard International, Singapore to Auk Chong GWEE, November 3, 2010.
[205] Email from Colin M to Leandra Ramm, December 22, 2010, 8:23 AM.
[206] Email from Stormo Rochalie to Leandra Ramm, December 22, 2010, 7:12 AM.
[207] Email from David Conceicao, ASP, Investigation Development Officer Ang Mo Kio Police Division, January 6, 2010.
[208] Email from Simi Horowitz, December 20, 2010, 10:39 AM.
[209] Email from Simi Horowitz, January 20, 2011, 12:04 PM.
[210] Email from Leandra Ramm to Lucinda Everett, March 18, 2011.
[211] Email excerpt from Miggy Miggy, March 29, 2010, 12:12 AM.
[212] Email excerpt from Stormo Rochalie to Gale Martin,

August 5, 2010, 12:00 AM.

[213] Email excerpt from Stormo Rochalie to Gale Martin, August 5, 2010, 12:02 AM.

[214] Email excerpt from Alexis Bowater to Leandra Ramm, March 13, 2011.

[215] *The Economist:* "Creepy crawlies: The Internet allows the malicious to menace their victims," April 20, 2011.

[216] See Appendix A for the Question and Answer emails between the *Economist* reporter and me, which was the foundation for the *Economist* article.

[217] Agent David Chaney

[218] Email extract from Leandra Ramm to The Blogger Team, September 13, 2011, 4:17 PM.

[219] http://stormorochalie.blogspot.com

[220] Email excerpt from Md Amirudin Md Abdullah March 11, 2012, 6:47 PM.

[221] Email excerpt from Eddie Tan - A.J. Fardella, March 26, 2012

[222] Email excerpt from A.J. Fardella, responding to Eddie Tan et al, March 26, 2012

[223] Email excerpt from A.J. Fardella to Eddit TAN (SPF), Mohammad Amirudin, copied to Gordon Jenkins (FBI), Daniel.Schott (US Secret Service) and former Secret Service Agent Tom Galligan, March 26, 2012.

[224] 2013 Email excerpt from A.J. Fardella to Mohamed Amirudin, copies to Chia Wei, Eddie Tan, Leandra Ramm, Brian Addington, Chief of Police, Pittsburg, Edgar Sanchez, Detective Pittsburg Police, Gordon Jenkins, FBI special agent, Secret Service Resident Agent In Charge and two others. Daniel Schott.